The Shape of Likelihood:
Relevance and the
University

THE SHAPE OF LIKELIHOOD: RELEVANCE AND THE UNIVERSITY

The Franklin Lectures in the Sciences and Humanities

Second Series

LOREN EISELEY
DETLEV W. BRONK
JACOB BRONOWSKI
HOWARD MUMFORD JONES

Preface by Taylor Littleton

Published for
AUBURN UNIVERSITY
by
THE UNIVERSITY OF ALABAMA PRESS
University, Alabama

THE FRANKLIN LECTURES IN THE SCIENCES & HUMANITIES
Edited by Taylor Littleton

FIRST SERIES: *Approaching the Benign Environment,*
by R. Buckminster Fuller, Eric A. Walker, James R. Killian, Jr.

SECOND SERIES: *The Shape of Likelihood: Relevance and the University.*
by Loren Eiseley, Detlev W. Bronk, Jacob Bronowski, Howard Mumford Jones.

COPYRIGHT © 1970 AND 1971 BY
THE UNIVERSITY OF ALABAMA PRESS,
except as follows:
"Protest and Prospect," COPYRIGHT © 1971
by Jacob Bronowski
Library of Congress Catalog Card Number 73–135709
International Standard Book Number 0–8173–6642–3
All rights reserved
Manufactured in the United States of America

Contents

Contributors

LOREN EISELEY, one of America's most highly respected social philosophers, is Benjamin Franklin Professor of Anthropology and the History of Science, University of Pennsylvania, and the author of a number of widely acclaimed works, including *The Immense Journey* (1957), *The Firmament of Time* (1960), and *The Unexpected Universe* (1969).

DETLEV BRONK, President of Rockefeller University since 1953, was formerly President of the National Academy of Sciences (1950–1962) and Chairman of the National Science Board of the National Science Foundation (1956–1964).

JACOB BRONOWSKI, since 1964 a Senior Fellow at the Salk Institute for Biological Research, is a historian and philosopher of science, statistician, interpreter of literature and contemporary culture, and poet, and the author of *Science and Human Values* (1956), *William Blake and the Age of Revolution* (1965), and *The Identity of Man* (1965).

HOWARD MUMFORD JONES, well known for his many distinguished contributions to American and English literary and cultural historiography, is the author of *Ideas in America* (1965), *Pursuit of Happiness* (1966), and many other books.

Preface

In the opening lines of Shakespeare's *Henry IV, Part 1*, the king, troubled by the civil strife lately abroad in the land, speaks of leading a unified force—a force marching "all one way"—to liberate the Holy Land:

> So shaken as we are, so wan with care,
> Find we a time for frighted peace to pant,
> And breathe short-winded accents of new broils
> To be commenced in strands afar remote.

But this desire to put the problems of England aside in favor of new, ostensibly noble "broils" elsewhere is frustrated by news of further discord in Wales and also in Scotland, where the noise of cannon and the "shape of likelihood" augur further internal violence for England.

Those entrusted with the care and sustenance of our universities in the 1970s may well appreciate and even share Henry's yearning for an end of internal strife and discord close to home—whether or not they share his taste for crusades "in strands afar remote." A realistic assessment of the situation on most campuses suggests, however, that for some time to come the fulfillment of the university's humane and social ideals must yet be pursued amid the sound and confusion of cultural confrontation and uncertain purposes. Even so, if we pursue our Shakespearean analogy a bit further, we recall that King Henry's stated desire for a noble crusade is not altogether true to his suspicious, guilt-ridden nature, and that the

vii

real hope for England's future lies in the generous and sensible temperament of his son Hal, the future Henry V. Could it be that the prospects of the university are not quite so dim as they may seem at first sight? After all, Hal's youthful indifference to matters which Henry considered serious and important sorely tried the father's patience, but the young prince did, in time, come to recognize and accept the lessons and burdens—the "relevance"—of the past. Is it not possible that some of the many and vociferous students who now attack universities as "irrelevant" may follow a similar course?

No mere literary analogy is likely to have much effect on real events, of course, but perhaps the one offered here will at least serve the useful purpose of reminding young and old alike that everyone who lives long enough is *both* young and old, and will suggest, further, that intellectual and moral judgments based solely on immediate appearances at any given moment are to be made, if at all, only with the utmost caution.

In this volume on the shape of likelihood in American higher education, four men of distinguished academic achievement consider the problem of student unrest and dissent and our quest for values in the light of both our developing experience as a nation and the wider life of man. Their individual analyses of the virtue of patience (in Emerson's use of the term), their recognition of the need for an ethical reform of the curriculum on modern foundations, their faith in the continuing relevance of history, science, and the imagination, and their confidence in the potential viability of the university in the society of the future, all should help us achieve a better and more sympathetic understanding of the student protests that have left more than a few of us somewhat "shaken as we are." And they should also help us to sustain our hopes that the current difficult times may yet contain the wisdom and power necessary, as Eiseley says, for us "to cross the surges of the future." They should help us all, young or old, to see that the shape of likelihood, though it be accompanied by the noise of cannon, is indeed promising—a shape, to return to Shakespeare's words, such as

> ... a man may prophesy,
> With a near aim, of the main chance of things
> As yet not come to life, which in their seeds
> And weak beginnings lie intreasured.

Auburn University   TAYLOR LITTLETON
March, 1971

Loren Eiseley

Introduction

Loren Eiseley

Introduction

To COMPOSE AN INTRODUCTION to this volume of addresses, given under the Franklin Foundation Lecture Series at Auburn University, is no small task. Two great scientists, at heart equally distinguished as humanists, and one internationally known student of literature, have, each in his own way, examined the forces of change at work in our society.

The accelerated influence of science on human life has been wisely noted by Dr. Bronk, who has glimpsed within our present confusion the potential dawn of a new science that may yet accord more fittingly with the dreams of the original seventeenth-century statesmen of science. Dr. Bronowski, in turn, has reminded us that revolt and change have always been part of the life of human societies and that when a whole system of values falls under challenge, as in the democratic West of our day, then only by the greater understanding of men and change can we avoid the dire polarizations that lead to irrational violence and confrontation. Finally, Howard Mumford Jones, in ranging over the past, has perceived that change in educational institutions has not always implied advance. Moreover, the capture of universities by anti-intellectual forces can spell imminent disaster. He does well to remind us of the dangers of always equating social turmoil with progress, or impatience with virtue. All these observations are pertinent to our time, and they are given further authority by the distinction and experience of their authors.

If there is some difference in the emphasis which they have assigned certain topics, its source doubtless lies in the individual experience of the scholar and the method of his approach. It will be noted that they agree on one thing: that change is running through the body politic like a fever. If it were not, they and others of their colleagues would not be caught up in such a common concern and distress.

It is no light matter to find oneself adrift in a society which appears increasingly to deny the values to which one has given a life-long allegiance. Moreover, because ours is a society responsive to the commercially oriented mass media, one is forced to ask, as in no other era, which of these many voices is real, which constitutes a tiny minority with a very loud trumpet, what is fad, what progress, what has come by devious routes from without, and what is genuinely indigenous protest from within.

That there are no very ready answers to these questions reveals how insidiously our present troubles came upon us. The intellectual weathers of a given period frequently escape the attention of the contemporary meteorologist until the storm has descended. I have heard our student rebellion ascribed to the discovery and use of atomic weapons, to the civil rights movement, to the Vietnam war, to the decline of religious faith, to the rise of an

4

affluent society of materialistic values and hedonistic morals—even to the rise of science itself. I disclaim none of these single observations, but I assert that the social scientists of a more removed century will undoubtedly discern roots lying deeper than these within our past. They will also, I believe, fail to find in the self-evaluating, self-imitating, self-rationalizing nature of man any single explanation for what, with very little preliminary evidence of unrest, has burst so suddenly upon us.

Men react to diverse stimuli. They are frequently poor judges of their own motivations, which are apt to prove multiple. We are frequently left in the realm of probabilities rather than in the domain of what might be called scientific causation. Our passions are reflected in other eyes. We bear within us a kind of mutual contagion, one more easily released in some circumstances than in others. Men enact, in short, imagined roles in front of mirrors.

There have been certain discussions of anthropological principles either directly or inferentially stated within the essays that follow. As an anthropologist I should like to review certain basic facts and concepts which may have a bearing on the events of our time. I do so neither as a complete analysis of our present predicament nor in contradiction to what has been ably said by others. My sole wish is to add, if possible, some observations upon man and his history that may contribute to the full picture of our time. I do so in the hope that as the reader comes to peruse the statements of the distinguished scholars represented here, he may find his judgment supported by a strong realization of the uniqueness of our present circumstances and the dangers implicit in any great urban civilization whose hold on the reality of its association with nature is slipping away. To say this of a scientifically oriented society may sound paradoxical. There is, however, a difference between the mastery of nature and respect for the powers of nature that are unmasterable by man. The first attitude leads to exploitation and ultimately to destruction of resources, the latter to a protective ethic of respect that primitive man has frequently understood better than our technologically oriented society. In the light of this observation, let us attempt to examine what may be regarded as the peculiar vulnerability of American society even though, as Dr. Bronowski has noted, the symptoms of psychological disturbance extend across national boundaries.

Not many years ago a very able student of folklore, Joseph Campbell, remarked that "the chronicle of our species from its earliest page, has been not simply an account of the progress of man, the toolmaker, but—more tragically—a history of the pouring of blazing visions into the minds of seers and the efforts of earthly communities to incarnate unearthly covenants."

"Unearthly covenants" is not an unapt description for some of the secular movements being diffused upon today's campuses. Although the vociferous prophets of these restless cults may proclaim themselves to be the most absolute of realists, they are frequently the confused spokesmen for visions—visions projected by other men in other times and hurried along in the unending stream of social change until circumstance gives them wide currency.

That without visions and imagination mankind would scarcely be the restless and adaptable creature that it is, we must immediately admit. On the other hand, from the time of the emergence of language itself man has possessed the uncanny power of symbolically reworking his

6

surrounding environment in his head. He can displace or transform the existent world for a prospective emergent reality reoriented in the mind. But that emergent reality can only be brought into being by enlisting, through speech or writing, the aid of other individuals.

The author of the General Epistle of James in the New Testament observed long ago that although the tongue is a little member it sets the course of nature on fire. Moreover, James fully recognized the ambivalent and frightening shapes that can be summoned up by language when he remarked that the tongue "can no man tame" and that it was capable of loosing deadly poison into the world. Thus, though man's full life is acquired and his culture and institutions transmitted by the word, speech has not been an unmitigated blessing. It can be lent to the lie as well as the truth. Men can distort or manipulate the meaning of words until, as in our time, such words as *relevance* and *confrontation,* to mention but two, begin to take on new overtones. *Relevance* in particular becomes endowed, in the mouths of the ignorant, with a narrow fanaticism that has well-nigh destroyed a once useful word.

When a college student can "confront" his professor, as one did recently, with the covert sneer "What is the relevance of evolution?," it is all too evident that a scarcely veiled hostility has replaced an objective interest in the origin and destiny of man. "Relevance," thus interpreted, reveals the worst aspects of the "Now" cult which flourishes upon our campuses. Such intellectual evasions, though offered under the guise of the new freedom, are as narrowly confining as the fanatical puritanism of an earlier day. Now still another factor confronts us—the impact of mass media. Granted the nature of

7

man's mind, his youthful hunger for novelty and the desire for "unearthly covenants," granted also the power of technological change to deepen the normal gap between the generations—then these instruments, lending themselves to voice and vision, can whip the hysteria of a new cult, a new mode of life, from one campus to another with incredible rapidity.

The animal body, built to receive stimuli and to react to them, has now become part of a body politic which receives such stimuli almost as fast as our individual nervous systems. What the communications specialist would call "background noise" mounts excessively. The individual in western society, and increasingly in all societies, is being subjected to more auditory and visual impact than he can successfully absorb. The result may be to dull our senses, at the same time that our own voices reach an unpleasant shouting pitch in the attempt to communicate.

The four-letter word, long banned from polite society, is utilized for its shock value upon the elder generation. Also, the word torrent from radio and television impairs, in too great quantity, the selectivity of reason, just as the deluge of enormous quantities of print finally dulls our response to this more traditional medium. Once more the eventual result is detrimental to quality. The lurid, the scatological, must be printed in bold type to stimulate weary senses. All of the fine promise of instant communication may in reality be endangered by an international electronic nerve-net whose powers of precipitation are vastly in excess of the average man's ability to absorb.

In a boiler factory one has to scream to be heard at all, and this is precisely what some of our domestic activity suggests today. A more sophisticated civilization may someday have to recognize that a satisfactory and unpunishing technology is one that does not subject the human nervous system to what it was never evolved to apprehend or endure. Man arose millions of years ago in small groups under wide skies and subject to great silences; in the last fifty years he has entered bedlam. He can produce by his mechanical devices more noise, even superficially meaningful noise, than his nerves were evolved to absorb. It is an aspect of pollution, not yet very fully comprehended, that may well play an increasing role in the social pathology of our time.

We are beginning to learn that in our first enthusiasm for control of outside nature we have forgotten the biological limitations of the creature inside. That creature is now showing symptoms of rejection of the entire apparatus he so confidently created. We would be wise not to ignore the irrationality of some of modern man's responses to his predicament. Instead we should enquire whether some aspects, at least, of our modern tantrums are an infantile response to noise levels beyond the ability of the species to long endure, particularly at its most impressionable age.

We might, in other words, join with Dr. Bronk in recognizing and trying to limit the misuses of science in order that it may never, by human neglect and indifference, be made to betray its creator.

Anything achieved by man has been created first by words, and words, as we have seen, partake of human ambivalence. Again in the words of James, from the same mouth proceed the blessing and the curse. The observation is just as germane to the field of science, for science is also subject to the frailties and fallibilities of all human endeavor.

Among the few persistent dreams of Western man one must recall the Arcadian—the dream of the renewed or rediscovered Eden—the innocent forest in which man may seek safety from the overwhelming complexities of civilization. It may seem strange to seek in the long American preoccupation with this dream some of the roots of today's difficulties, yet I believe a case can be made for a serious degree of connection. For many decades the young American republic lay hidden under the green canopy of the Eastern forest. It was largely unreachable by the European powers. Our leaders discouraged embroilment in foreign affairs and the open land to the west was extolled as the solution to class struggle and poverty. Man, American man, was entering upon a new destiny largely devoid of history and its sad reversals. In the wilderness he would be purified; the moving frontier would perpetuate the rugged virtues of an egalitarian society.

The whole range of this philosophy was well expressed by the late historian Walter Prescott Webb. He observes, in *The Great Frontier*: "Looked at in the long perspective, the Utopias offer evidence of the existence of a point of view and a philosophical concept that is modern. In general they assume that progress can be made ... that human perfectibility is attainable and worth striving for. The new abundance of wealth had enabled men to make real progress in economic affairs. Science and criticism had eaten away the pillars of superstition and unreasoning faith. ... If by his own wit man could conquer the material world, why could he not control and direct himself and his fellows? A little thought," continued Webb, "would have shown him the magnitude of the last task in comparison with the first one. The material world which

10

he was conquering was inanimate and did not talk back
... or have other plans of its own."

For a time, for perhaps the first century of the national
dream, the ax, the long rifle, and the covered wagon may
stand as symbols. As one of Steinbeck's characters says in
The Red Pony: "It was a whole bunch of people made
into one big crawling beast.... It was westering and
westering. Every man wanted something for himself, but
the big beast that was all of them wanted only westering.
... When we saw the mountains at last, we cried—all of
us. But it wasn't getting here that mattered it was movement and westering."

Finally the old man says to his grandson's questionings:
"No place to go, Jody.... But that's not the worst—no,
not the worst. Westering has died out of the people.
Westering isn't a hunger any more. It's all done."

In anger the boy's father cries out, "All right! Now it's
finished. Nobody wants to hear...."

But is it really finished? That is the question that seems
to hover unspoken in the eyes of American youth. It is
true we have come to the sea. It is true that the physical
westering is done, and that our still expanding population
increasingly concentrates in the great block cities. Nevertheless, if the westering is not a hunger anymore, something curious has replaced it: the wing and the wheel.
We are the most restless, mobile, and rootless people on
earth, and our youth extend the pattern. Ancestrally we
are the offscourings and rejects of all the ports of Europe,
the workers who dug the Erie canal or wandered, looking
for gold, through the high passes of the Sierras. Now the
night never quite closes on the lights streaming along the
highways of America.

"Forget it. It's finished. No one wants to hear," cried

11

the man desperate to erase the past. Strangely, like something fixed in the blood, modern youth is beginning to remember an equivalent for westering. I do not believe that all its storm and violence is quite compounded of today, however much the young may imagine this to be so. I do not believe that it is all a product of the latest catchwords and slogans. In the 1930s youth drifted jobless in a vast uneasy current on the freight trains between the coasts; youth rejected security and many died under the wheels. Dreaming in isolationist splendor of the old green canopy, it marched and died and became disillusioned in the great wars of this century—the wars that had been entered upon belatedly because each time they had seemed to deny the safety of the remembered forest. Moreover, they had drawn the escaped prisoner back into the uncomfortable domain of history.

Sometime after the close of the Second World War and in the midst of what has come to be known as the Cold War, I can remember the sudden outburst of a former naval officer and businessman as we sat exchanging confidences in a bar in Manhattan. With an abruptness of manner that revealed his inner tensions, this man, who had come originally from the west, cried out, "Why do we have to go on paying taxes to support a United Nations which has never kept the peace anywhere? Why do we have to keep doling out money to people who secretly hate and despise us all over the world? This has gone on for ten years after a war we were supposed to have won. America is tired, tired, I tell you. We're sick of it."

The words of Steinbeck's character came back to me. "All right! Now it's finished. Nobody wants to hear. . . ."

Again, in other circumstances, another friend of my generation, of the war years, cried furiously, hurling his coat upon the floor, "I tell you America is being black-mailed by the entire world."

This is not the forum in which to try to decide whether these men were right or wrong. But their emotions were very real and they long preceded and should have con-stituted a warning upon the remote adventure of Viet-nam. I could only try to explain to my friends the blunt fact that America had reentered history, that the green forest was no longer a satisfactory defense line, and that wars, alas, never remained settled like the box scores of athletic games.

Of one thing only am I sure—that in tears of frustra-tion these fighting men of another generation did not hear me. I could not appease them. Perhaps in the end it was only their children who had heard, their children of the good green land with no history but that of the westering, the romantic history that disclaims all history. We must, however, recapitulate what that history implied: it extolled man's ability to progress and placed its faith in human perfectibility. As the great westering animal came down to the water's edge it turned 'round upon itself in dismay. The day of urban concentrations and in-creasing social stratification had begun.

Yet there remained in the great animal a sense of well-being and enormous power. Inventions made for the frontier, the Colt revolver and the Conestoga wagon, gave way to steam and concentrated industry. My own father, in his declining years, still spoke wistfully of getting a little "passel" of cheap land and would send for circulars offering wild, uncleared acreage in the Ozarks. We of the younger generation would speak amusedly of papa's "rab-bit farm," the Rousseauian retreat of his old age.

But even we talked in symbolic terms of frontiers—

frontiers of science, frontiers of business opportunity, frontiers of education. The National Aeronautics and Space Administration, NASA, has cunningly used the "frontiers of space" in its public appeal for support of the moon project. The great land of unhistory in which we strove to hide has turned, in other words, into a country of drama, some good, some bad, but all in one sense or another still linked to the Arcadian myth. Not least of these is education. The federal government alone, Webb has noted, allotted sufficient land for educational purposes to make a band of earth eight miles wide that would circle the equator, with another enormous stretch left over. Only the great frontier made this possible, and only the great "westering animal," with its faith in perfectibility and "know how," would have left such a spoor behind it.

In those institutions the dream unconsciously continued; the philosopher and political scientist dreamed of perfecting individual man and society. The scientist groped amidst raw outside nature so that it might be tamed and transported. On a thread of wire the electric power generated by great rivers enters our living room. Computers of incredible complexity compress the mathematics of a human lifetime into instants and hurl a rocket across the freezing void to Mars.

Notable among our experiments in outer space is a life style unconsciously different from that which our competitors have shown. This is the "fly by." Naturally we have wanted our instruments to record to the last, but where the Russians have chosen to crash land a vehicle as if to establish "first presence," a frontier evasiveness has determined many of our efforts. We have photographed, and flown the vehicle on, on, until the radio became a whisper and the great void of space received and silenced our probe of its immensities. All systems were "go" until contact could reach no farther. Even then, in imagination, we ride, as did Jedediah Smith, the first westering frontiersman, who came down the Sierra ranges into California so long ago.

We are not, in short, a sedate stop-over people, and this has been both our advantage and our weakness. Our numbers grow. We cannot all venture out among the starfields or climb the heights of the industrial frontiers we are so glibly assured afford us equal opportunity. We hunger for space but shrink from the entangling foreign wars and alliances that the elder statesmen of our new Arcadia so eloquently cautioned us against entering upon, ever. Because we have held to a great faith in human perfectibility and reason, we have by gifts and generous gestures sought to be loved, and frequently encountered hatred. We have thought our romantic concepts of democracy would be readily accepted by all newborn states. We have been disappointed. Even at home the somewhat nebulous new-found word "pluralism" threatens to become more popular than "Americanism," in some circles. The westering beast is threatening to fragment itself, yet the symptoms at the core remain.

Yesterday on the campus of my university I encountered a covered wagon drawn by two old horses. At the back of the wagon students were gathering, fascinated by a display of broad, handmade leather belts and similar accoutrements. Only the Colt six-shooter was missing. More and more girls and boys are appearing in fringed leather jackets and trousers, their shoulder-length hair held in place with banded beads. On the California coast road on an Easter holiday I have seen lines of these students with packs and bedrolls drifting aimlessly like stragglers on Napoleon's retreat from Moscow. Numbers of them take their degrees, abandon the cities, and drift into the communes that sound remarkably like one aspect of earlier American experience—the Utopian community, whether religious or intellectual.

It has occasionally been said that these extremes represent post-historic man, man already anticipating his end and returning to the wilderness. I would call the phenomenon more complex than this. I would contend that these youngsters so subject to the rolling wheel, so intent upon a new life style, are not the subject of any post-Hiroshima trauma whatever. They are not leaving history; they are trying to reenter it on their own terms. What they do not consciously realize is that the history they seek to reenact is that of the westering beast which disclaimed all history but its own. The communes are not new, the demands for "relevance" are a kind of uncouth parody of the western pragmatism which rejected everything that could not practicably be carried west with the wagons—the cult, that is, of the Now.

The weariness of the angry forest culture so fitfully expressed by my comrades of the forties—the disillusion of the Cold War, the reentrance into that history where no real detente exists but only the ebb and flow of giant power—has now been complicated by another facet of the lost forest world. It is the belief in the noble savage, the conception that in the rejection of material comfort, the mortification of the flesh, some kind of spiritual perfection is engendered.

The always somewhat specious industrial frontier has given way, under our thickening crust of technological achievement, to a renewed search for an inward frontier of personal experience. That it has resulted in all manner of drug experimentation and something of a sexual revolution might have been predicted. That all cults of rejection are apt to erupt into outrageous caricatures of virtue goes without saying—the young castigating their parents and the parents holding horrified and guilt-ridden post-mortems over the younger generation.

In reality, both generations are caught in the timeless historical embrace of a vanished forest and a great journey that is not ever to be repeated on the planet. We expected my father's generation to be the last to dream of the rabbit farm as an escape. This happens not to be true. Besides the violence of occasional traitors and psychopaths masking themselves self-righteously in the garb of peace, there is now the cult of the genuine flower people, the seekers for that Eden the western marchers both paradoxically believed in and destroyed. Perhaps cultures, like individual men, are destined always to betray themselves and then endlessly to relive their bereavement. Such grief and such frustration may be visited, however unfairly, upon the fathers. In a time when national boundaries appear less permanent than ideologies, there is much room for worry. The hidden dreams of a culture are never finished, however much adults may cry out that they are.

Steinbeck's little boy Jody timidly asked his westering grandfather if possibly boats might be an answer. The old man replied sadly that there was no place left to go. It is true that the westering animal, the great American beast, has nowhere to go and has almost destroyed its Eden. Long ago, however, Plato had ventured that we must choose carefully, like a shipwrecked wanderer, upon what shakily constructed raft of ideas we would risk the voyage of life.

I am an American of the end of the westering time. I think that Jody's idea of a boat is good but that it must be a boat of ideas not endlessly symbolizing our strange, irreplaceable, "historyless" past. I believe we must try to think further, wisely, and with a true knowledge that though our forefathers came to the New continent wishing to forget the Old, it followed them. The history of man is always relevant and it is inescapable. From it is drawn the future, even the future that troubles us now. The "boat" imagined by little Jody has already been partially constructed by those pioneers who scattered schools prodigally behind them as if they presciently knew that someday they would be needed. They are the only rafts we have, and if they fail us, then all the westering has been in vain.

It is for this reason the papers in this volume should be read so carefully. They will not contain all that we must understand to survive, but their authors, who are mature and patient scholars, would be the last to reject the intellectual frontier. They would merely say, as to the small boy Jody, that a boat to cross the surges of the future must be well made by craftsmen who do not reject either tradition or innovation. They know, however, the burden of the passage. They do not confuse everything that is new with progress. They know that Americans are a peculiar people who have lived and are living through a unique experience, and that the shapes of vanished trees hang over us and are part of the tradition that sets our young men of the mid-twentieth century to wearing buckskins. But clothing and the shouted word "relevance" will not in the end suffice. We must learn to know ourselves, our past, our own true hunger, and where the real frontier we seek lies waiting. Little Jody's dream of a boat may contain the truth if we take it as a hopeful symbol. Surely both Plato and a child could scarce be wrong.

Detlev W. Bronk

The Nature of Science and Its Humane Values

Parts of "The Nature of Science and Its Humane Values" by Detlev W. Bronk appeared in the 1971 *Britannica Yearbook of Science and the Future,* published by The Encyclopedia Britannica, Inc., by permission of The University of Alabama Press.

Detlev W. Bronk

The Nature of Science and Its Humane Values

IN THESE TIMES when the theme of my discourse is crucial to the survival of modern civilization, I deem it an especial privilege to speak under the auspices of the foundation established at Auburn University by John Leonard Franklin. Mr. Franklin devoted his life to the application of scientific knowledge for the material needs of mankind. And Auburn University was founded as a land-grant college to "teach such branches of learning as are related to agriculture and the mechanic arts . . . without excluding other scientific studies." Those are still worthy endeavors for men and institutions, despite the rising clamor of many who decry science and technology as causes of the undesirable qualities of modern life.

Science and technology have indeed enabled men and women and even children to do things that harm themselves and others and make life generally undesirable in city slums, on crowded highways through desecrated countrysides, in Biafra and Indochina, everywhere. But without the use of science and technology, how could man survive on our overcrowded planet?

21

This would not deserve question or comment were not the clamor so loud and the critics of science so numerous, even among scholars and men of affairs, that the President's Task Force on Science Policy has been moved to report: "The Nation . . . needs to insure that the effectiveness of our science and technology is not downgraded or destroyed by the unthinking or the uninformed. . . . The rapid rise of attitudes disdainful of science and technology, and the disillusionment of many young people with science and technology, is of grave concern."

During thirty years on the frontiers between science, technology, and public affairs I have pondered the causes of this growing disdain of science. I have found three that are prevalent and deeply rooted: lack of understanding of the nature of science, loss of individual identity in the creative use of science, the misuse of science and technology. These I will discuss.

Because the nature of the scientific endeavor and the social forces that determine how scientific knowledge is used are so little understood, science and technology have an ambivalent status in society today. To an increasing degree our health and comfort and our very survival depend on scientific knowledge and its applications. The people of poor "under-developed countries" crave the products of advanced technology that could make their lives more healthy, secure, and desirable. Affluent nations use science and technology to defend and extend the material benefits they have acquired from science-based industries. Why, then, does a prominent statesman say: "Today we stand helpless before the onslaught of science." Does he indeed mean that we stand helpless before the onslaught of *knowledge*?

Science is, surely, knowledge gained in man's endless quest for understanding. Or so I have thought ever since my student days at Michigan, when I wrote to my father: "Each of five nights a week through two happy years has been a night of high adventure in my basement laboratory room. A moving spot of light, reflected from a galvanometer that measures the properties of molecules in a gas, has led me on as sailors are led by stars through unknown waters. Night after night I watch the hours pass on the lighted clock in the campus tower. At five o'clock comes the morning's first trolley with disturbances that halt my work. No matter to you what I learn during the long nights, it will be written in dusty journals. What matters much to you and me is that I have savored the endless joy of discovering something new. In the dingy basement my path in life has come clear."

My philosopher-father was pleased, for such thoughts were consistent with his belief in the spiritual quality of science. He liked to quote his literary friend John Livingston Lowes, who wrote in *The Road to Xanadu*: "The leap of the imagination, in a garden at Woolsthorpe on a day in 1665, from the fall of an apple to an architectonic conception cosmic in its scope and grandeur, is one of the dramatic moments in the history of human thought."

Those are not rare, esoteric concepts of science written in the enthusiasm of youth or in the cloistered study of a literary scholar. After a lifetime that continues on the pinnacles of scientific achievement and recognition, Nobel physicist I. I. Rabi writes: "One of the greatest rewards of the pursuit of scientific discovery ... may come in an illuminating flood of insight or in the course of an experiment.... Although scientists don't write about these moments of exultation and ecstasy ... these fleeting visions can in one flash reward one for years of patient and exhausting work. At these times the scientist is filled with profound awe and humility that such wonders should be revealed through him. There is a quality about science, or rather about nature, which is always miraculous in its originality. To obtain a glimpse of this wonder can be the reward of a lifetime. This itself can be the sufficient satisfaction of the aspiration which makes scientists scientists."

Rabi and I have been associated for years in many endeavors wherein science has been applied for human use and social ends. Those practical employments, even the building of our military defenses, have not shaken our faith that the basic mission of science is the quest for order and beauty and deeper understanding.

The acquisition of knowledge does not need the justification of usefulness: its true sanction is inherent in itself. We are too prone to torment ourselves with devising far-fetched reasons; we should be content with the simple truth asserted by Aristotle: "All men possess by nature a craving for knowledge." Curiosity, the desire to know things as they are, the desire for understanding are born with every man. It is a craving no less native to the being of man, no less universal than the craving for food and drink. If that craving is denied satisfaction, the spirit of man is starved; in the words of Plato, "part of him dies and he never attains completeness and health, but walks lame to the end of his life."

That unique spiritual quality of man, distinguishing him from all other living creatures, is the basic motive of the scientific endeavor by which modern man has evolved from the savage. Because constant change accompanies intellectual and social evolution, timid and reactionary forces try to suppress that deeply rooted human attribute.

This threat to freedom for inquiry has been most violent during times of rapid social change that severely taxes the adaptable spirit of man. Because it is true of the present, J. H. Plumb, Professor of Modern History at Cambridge, pertinently says: "one of the most distressing aspects of our own time has been the growth of anti-intellectualism and the flight from reason in those circles where it ought to be most intensely cultivated."

But denial of the humane value of scientific knowledge and suppression of its wise use for the benefit of man is certainly not unique to our time. Two hundred years ago Voltaire deplored "the astonishing contrasts" of his time: "reason on the one hand, the most absurd fanaticism on the other . . . sauve qui peut."

History is replete with records of opposition to scientific inquiry, to new knowledge and new technologies that shattered old beliefs and changed patterns of life. Servetus, Galileo, and Darwin are classic examples of scientists whose inquiries, discoveries, and theories were opposed and suppressed by irrational prejudice. The fate of Vavilov, who dared oppose Lysenko, is a recent reminder that the pressure of mistaken government priorities can suppress knowledge for a while with consequences that are disastrous for a nation. And the present rejection of scientific research as a means for improving the quality of life could have especially serious social consequences because of the vital role of science in modern society.

Scientific teaching and research are now seldom curbed by religious opposition, physical force, or superstitious fear. When scientific endeavor is discouraged and research restrained, it is likely to be the consequence of social scorn or inadequate financial support.

Competence for a career in science requires long years of costly training. By controlling financial support of higher education, students are granted or denied the opportunity to pursue careers in science; the supply of scientists and those who apply science for social needs is thus determined for years to come. Much of modern research is costly; accordingly, the allocation of funds by government, industry, and foundations determines what research is done and who may do it. Withholding funds for education, for the salaries of scientists, and for the purchase of instruments can thus effectively suppress freedom for inquiry. The furtherance of science, therefore, depends largely upon public understanding of science and its role and status in society. This was said by President Kennedy at the Centennial of the National Academy of Sciences: "If basic research is to be properly regarded, it must be better understood. Together, the scientific community, the Government, industry, and education must work out the way to nourish science in all its power and vitality."

Science was not always remote from Everyman. I have lived much of my life in the industrial city of Philadelphia. I do not know how large a part science has in the thoughts of the two million who live there today; very little, I would say, if I were to judge by the space devoted to science in the newspapers of that city. And yet it was within the radius of no more than a quarter of a mile in the little Philadelphia of two hundred years ago that Benjamin Franklin and scores of its citizens in all walks of life took an active interest in science and contributed to its advancement.

To quote my historian friend Dean Nichols of the University of Pennsylvania: "The Philadelphians of the eighteenth century were engaged in discussing electricity, gravity, the transit of Venus, and other questions in basic science which did not have much immediate application, but because they wanted to satisfy their curiosity. Basic science was something of a community project eliciting general interest."

The twentieth century is not the eighteenth century, and we cannot bring back the relatively simple science of the age of Jefferson and Franklin. It is not often now that an amateur can make significant scientific discoveries; the furtherance of science depends upon highly trained professionals with access to expensive facilities and to colleagues in other sciences and distant countries. And so Dean Nichols, the historian, concludes: "Scientists must be more anxious to excite the imagination, the curiosity, and the hope of a somewhat frightened society. The times demand an effort to show to the community the values which may be conserved and insured by adequately supported programs in basic science. Our fellow men, by and large, are dazzled by the extent and complexity of our knowledge, they have no comprehension of the extent of what we do not know."

Fortunately, established scientific principles, the significance of the more important scientific discoveries, and the nature of scientific inquiry can still be stated with clarity and simplicity for the non-scientific reader. For this we need synthesizing architects of scientific concepts such as Professor Eiseley, also a contributor to this series, who has with clarity and grace built facts and data into the structure of knowledge. One does not envision a temple by looking at scattered bricks.

Scientists have too seldom heeded the advice given by President Kennedy: "If basic research is to be properly regarded, it must be better understood." And scientists have too seldom explained the nature of their endeavor as Havelock Ellis did that of Leonardo: "In the vast orbit in which he moved, the distinction between the artist and the scientist had little or no existence. . . . The medium in which the artist worked was Nature, in which the scientist works; every problem was to Leonardo a problem in science, every problem in physics to be approached in the spirit of the artist."

Here again I am reminded of a passage in *The Road to Xanadu*: "The imagination is not a bright but ineffectual faculty with which in some esoteric fashion scientists, poets and their kind are especially endowed. It is of the utmost moment that we recognize the essential oneness of its function and its ways with all the creative endeavours through which human brains, with dogged persistence, strive to discover and realize order in a chaotic world."

That was the humane hope in science of which Professor Rabi spoke at the Centennial of the National Academy of Sciences, as he was discussing the nature of science: "Over and above all this too human confusion is the assurance that with further study will come order and beauty and a deeper understanding."

In the meantime people are confused by sudden and radical changes in patterns of living, in customs and social structures, that seem to be caused by science and technology; they are frustrated by their individual inability to comprehend and control the forces of science and technology.

The average man's range of knowledge is greater now

than in the past, but his share of the total body of knowledge is far less. This is a consequence of specialism.

Because of the restrictive needs of the specialist, much of education, much of communication through mass media, and most books on science deal with facts and data more than with the meaning and significance of facts and data; there is more emphasis on the accumulation of facts than on the ability to comprehend them.

The growing demand and, yes, the increasing need for specialized knowledge rather than for a wide spectrum of knowledge is fostered by the accelerating increase of scientifically derived knowledge and the narrowing scope of human comprehension. The far-ranging minds of Leonardo and Thomas Jefferson took as their province the total knowledge of mankind. In the rich soil of wide knowledge their wisdom grew. This is less possible for modern scholars and men of affairs, who lose the capacity to see the larger purposes of what they do and how they are influenced by new scientific concepts and new technologies. Intellectual leaders and the managers of our social systems have become so specialized that they rely on groups of other specialists assembled in "Think Tanks"; there is a widening pattern of government and corporate management by committees.

Scholars, and universities too, are overwhelmed by the vast volume of scientific knowledge. Educators choose the easy way of the specialist rather than meet the exacting demands of a widely ranging, deeply questing scholar. The minds of students are molded by lectures that are usually dictations of winnowed facts; too seldom are students encouraged to learn by reading and by provocative discussions between student and teacher.

The forces of technological change and specialization

29

are not all and always impediments to broad learning.

For instance, the electronic storage and retrieval of facts in libraries of data make possible a wider synthesis of knowledge. This they do by marshalling a vast assemblage of facts with which man may think. They free men from the drudgery of search for information so that they have more time for thought over a wider range of knowledge.

I hear my pragmatic, utilitarian friends say that the restricted life of modern, urban man, who is isolated from a wide range of natural forces, provides little *use* for a wide range of knowledge. It is true that restricted need for divers talents and interests does not encourage wide learning. And it is true that there are many competent scientists and scholars whose interests and knowledge are specialized and restricted within narrow boundaries; they have been enabled to develop their competence by concentration. The pioneer is otherwise. I know of no scientists who are considered first rate who do not have broad interests which they satisfy by wide reading; they are the exceptions who lead specialists into new realms of knowledge and understanding.

It is true that the circumscribed lives of most people in our modern industrial society provide narrowly restricted opportunities for use of a broad range of knowledge. But when the responsibilities and power of each citizen in a democratic society are considered, the need for general knowledge is very great indeed.

Here lies deep frustration and dissatisfaction with the consequence of surging science and technology. The capabilities of mankind have been vastly augmented, but no one man alone encompasses and possesses those augmented powers. That was the deep meaning of the historic sentence Neil Armstrong spoke as he placed his foot upon the moon: "That is one small step for a man, one giant leap for all mankind."

When man first learned to use a lever, the power he could exert was increased forever; he needs the assistance of no one other than himself. The force exerted by the man who controls a nuclear device is vastly greater, but it is derived from a far-flung system of men and women who design and build and operate the generator and the distribution system.

Ancient man communicated with another by signal fires. Now man can see distant objects by television and hear voices from afar by Telestar. Distant vision and quick audition are made possible by many engineers and mammoth corporations.

One pioneer could build and paddle a canoe on voyages of exploration. The exploring astronauts travel farther, much farther, but their satellites are built and controlled by many, many others.

A giant leap by mankind enables one man to take an historic step.

Lone man becomes ever more dependent upon many others.

And so it is not surprising that the young people who are to live by technology should wish to reshape the social system so that each individual may have identity and greater dignity.

At the beginning of the age of experimental science three centuries ago, The Royal Society of London received its charter "For Improving Natural Knowledge." A century later the American Philosophical Society was founded in Philadelphia on the frontiers of an undeveloped continent "For Promoting Useful Knowledge." There has been endless discussion regarding the nature and relations of these two objectives: of pure and applied science, of basic science and technology. Certainly the first feeds the second and the latter stimulates the first. As for their several roles in society, Lord Adrian wisely commented at the four hundredth anniversary of Francis Bacon's birth: "It is not cant to put truth above comfort, but most of us would like both if we could get them and Bacon's plan set forth in the 'New Atlantis' aimed at both, for he held these to be inseparable." But it is characteristic of our unsettled times to question what is "comfort." That is the concern of Nigel Calder in his recent book *Social Control of the Uses of Science.* He decides "there is nothing that men should not know, but some things they should not do with their knowledge." Who is to decide what they may do with their knowledge? Certainly scientists are not infallible or omnipotent.

It is irrational to restrict a scientist to research the ultimate value and use of which he can predict. No one can predict the ultimate use of knowledge. The consequence of technology is more predictable, but its design and course usually follow the needs and desires of society. Science and technology make possible the present and future quality of life; social forces determine what it is and will be. Alone, scientists and those who apply science can seldom shape the pattern and quality of life.

Man has acquired vast new sources of energy, new means of movement and communication; his range of perception is far extended. If we are to employ these new powers for the benefit of man, we must develop social controls. And scientists must be more active in

32

guiding the use of their achievements for humane ends.

In the fields of public health, in ecology and conservation, in the esthetic design of machines, in accident prevention, in every sector of technology there is crucial and urgent need for use of biological science. Science has increased the years between birth and death of most people throughout the world. But we need constantly to ask ourselves whether more scientific knowledge could not be used more wisely to enrich the lives that are lived over the longer span of years. Man's scientific achievements have made possible more than mere survival.

During the course of centuries, man evolved gradually in an environment that changed slowly except in times of catastrophe. This is no longer true. By the use of scientific knowledge men can now alter their surroundings rapidly and radically. They can move quickly into environments in which man has never lived before; into outer space. Man can make his environment what he will as he has done in heated and air-conditioned buildings, in pressurized airplane cabins, in space capsules. This has profound implications for his future.

Our early ancestor gradually moved from caves to rude huts to cold houses of rough hewn stone. For countless centuries he warmed himself before open fires. The building industry has not been the most notable example of the application of science to the satisfaction of human desires, but within a century man has learned to build for himself land-saving, towering structures he ascends without effort.

Throughout recorded history and until about a century ago, men moved on their own legs. They gradually learned to travel a little faster and more easily by harnessing animals to carts on skids or wheels; boats were ultimately propelled by the force of wind on sails. In the short space of a century and a half, man has increased his speed of travel from no more than he could run to greater than the velocity of sound. He can encompass the globe within a few brief hours.

Man used to adapt his life to natural surroundings and lived in close association with other living creatures. Only slowly did he change the world as he found it: laboriously he cleared the forests with his axe, drained the swamps with shovel-dug ditches, hunted wild beasts, and endured the insects. Within the last few years, chainsaws fell trees across denuded acres, bulldozers change the earth's configuration, chemical insecticides quickly change the pattern of the fauna.

We are able to alter our environment ever more rapidly. But we are still living human creatures, little different from our ancestors of centuries ago. The laws of nature are the same, and we are part of nature. If we are wise, we will heed Francis Bacon: "The only way to master nature is to obey her." To that, J. Donald Adams, formerly book editor of *The New York Times*, has appropriately added: "Man has been diligent and profoundly intelligent in discovering what some, at least, of nature's laws are. We do not know, and may never know them all, but what is far more disturbing is that we have tried to transcend some of those that we do know."

Our increasing power to change the physical world around us, to build things and create new patterns of life, is due in large part to our machines. They are so numerous and powerful that few people think of them as the "evolutionary" development of the human organism. This they are. Instruments and machines have no function other than for human use. In the course of evolution

34

organisms have been developed whose relations to their physical environment differ greatly. But by the use of machines and by the creation of controlled environments suitable to his survival, man, more than any other form of life, has been able to extend quickly the natural powers he acquired slowly through organic evolution.

Many of the scientific discoveries from which these human advantages are derived have required the use of instrumental aids to the senses. Although the direct action of radiant energy and mechanical forces on sensory nerve cells has revealed many natural phenomena, it is by the instruments of modern science that we have gained much of our evidence of the universe in which we live. Such instruments are devices with which we increase the sensitivity, range, and discrimination of our senses. This is done by the concentration or amplification of energy, or by the transformation of one form of energy to another which is more delicately perceived. Through the medium of such instruments man has gained a more acute awareness of his environment. Through such instruments our intellectual horizons have been widened.

The trains of sensory events thus initiated may ultimately evoke intellectual processes leading to an understanding of natural phenomena. That, in turn, has stimulated the invention of machines for increasing human powers. By these our voice is carried around the world. The power of a hundred thousand horses is held under the control of a finger capable of releasing men from the bondage of labor. Machines carry us swiftly across the land, under the sea, and through the air. By machines we have created our surroundings without regard for natural heat or cold, light or darkness.

One of the dissatisfactions with science today is the misuse of resulting technology for the domination and exploitation of poorer countries by those having greater resources of scientific knowledge, research, and technical competence. The dissatisfaction is especially and widely prevalent among our idealistic youth.

There are no national boundaries of science. The properties of matter and the behavior of living organisms under controlled conditions are not affected by the limits of states. Natural phenomena observed anywhere fit into a consistent pattern valid everywhere. That is the basis for the worldwide unity of science.

When a scientist considers the social usefulness of his accomplishments, he realizes that he is truly a citizen of the world. A new chemical agent for the treatment of disease is of potential benefit to all men. The laws of electromagnetic induction discovered by Faraday, an Englishman, have eased the labors of people in many countries. The observations of Galileo and Copernicus and Newton have widened the intellectual horizons of most people in all nations.

And yet it is a tragic characteristic of these days that there is a great and growing gap between those who have knowledge and adequate material resources and those who have not, between affluent and poor nations.

There are many reasons for the widespread and deep poverty, ignorance, and disease found in many countries of Africa, Asia and Latin America: inadequate natural resources, over-population, illiteracy, incompetent government, little support of scientific research and development. Always, a basic cause is a "technological gap" between them and the more prosperous nations.

Until recently there has been little appreciation of the

role and significance of science in modern society by those who determine national policies in "underdeveloped countries." Consequently, there has been a woeful lack of support of scientific and technical education, of laboratories for scientific research and industrial development. There is inadequate use of scientists, engineers, and physicians in schools and colleges, in government, and in the private sectors of agriculture and industry.

The results have been inflexible and unproductive agriculture, industries that are unable to satisfy domestic needs and are inadequate to provide sufficient exports, low standards of living and poor health, need for humiliating foreign assistance.

With a long tradition of internationalism, scientists will not remain indifferent to the fate of sister nations in which the great majority of people are in abject poverty, under-nourished, barely literate, facing a grim future that may be even worse than the present. Unless we close the "gap," our humane tradition will be degraded, and the world we have so largely shaped will not be free to trade the necessities and goods of life. It will be a world in which "peace" will be maintained only by military and economic domination, a world in which destructive revolutions will prevent progressive evolution toward a better quality of life.

That need not be, for as President Kennedy said in his address to the Academy of Sciences, from which I have already quoted, "science is the most powerful means we have for the unification of knowledge, and a main obligation of its future must be to deal with problems which cut across boundaries, whether boundaries between the sciences, boundaries between man's scientific and his humane concern, or boundaries between nations."

There is one supreme threat to the future welfare of all countries; science is deeply involved as both cause and possible corrective. It cuts across boundaries between nations, and it is the utmost challenge to technology. I refer, of course, to the irrational use of man's power to create human life.

Science and technology have enabled mankind to achieve so much, and so rapidly, that the limits of a finite earth are too often ignored. By the use of improved agricultural techniques, somewhat more people can be provided with adequate food for life. Atomic fuel added to other sources of health and power will satisfy the needs of many more people for warmth and the manufacture of things. Shelter for increasing populations can be provided by building higher. There are still some parts of the surface of the earth on which a man can walk about without pressing against others. There is still some land and air and water not yet polluted by enough human products to destroy life. But for how long?

Here are familiar statistics and predictions. From the beginning of recorded history until 1850, man increased in number to one billion. During the subsequent seventy-five years we multiplied our kind to two billion in 1925; to three billion in 1960 and, as we go, to four billion in 1975. We seem determined to continue on to five billion in 1985, six billion in 1994, and seven billion in 2000. So we go into another century, faster and faster toward an infinity of people.

But if a man can be put on the moon, some people have wondered, why cannot technology cope with the needs of ever-increasing population? Perhaps it can—and I fear that it will. Ultimately, further growth may be limited by the overheating our descendants will produce!

As we approach that limit, what will be the *quality* of life?

Dissatisfaction with the *present* quality of life may turn out to be our salvation. It may foster greater unity of the sciences and lead scientists back into closer associations with others engaged in humane endeavors. It may arouse throughout society a sense of responsibility for wise and humane use of the powers science has conferred upon man. Those who decry the "materialism" of modern life may be persuaded to use science and technology for spiritual and esthetic ends.

For scientists and technologists can do more than improve the material conditions of life. They are partners of many others who seek to satisfy man's craving for spiritual and emotional satisfactions. The technological recording of sound has preserved the transient artistry of the musician and has given to many the best music, until quite recently accessible only to the few. Modern methods of communication facilitate exchange of thought between those who are widely separated, and transportation expands the scope of social contacts. Technology can free men from the bonds of debilitating labor for mere survival and thus enable some to produce works of creative art and many to enjoy it as auditors and spectators. The technology of flight enables us to view scenes of beauty as we look down upon sculptured clouds above blue waters. Technologists provide new materials with which to evolve new forms of graphic art, architecture, and sculpture.

In *This Slum of a Decade,* Richard Rovere, a perceptive commentator on the national scene, expresses this cautious optimism: "If things work out as I hope they will, but deeply fear they won't, I can see someone looking back on this decade a decade from now, or two, or three, and seeing in it a period of great enlightenment and progress. It could be a great turning point in many ways ... the decade in which science made the greatest and most life-serving advances in human history. Adversity may still have its sweet uses."

After fifty years as an engineer, biologist, and servant of universities and government, I still have faith in science and reason as sure means for creating an ever better quality of life. Relevant to this faith are these lines from Lucretius:

> Our terrors and our darkness of
> mind
> Must be dispelled ...
> ... by insight into nature, and by
> a scheme
> Of systematic contemplation.

And the already-quoted confidence of Rabi: "Over and above all this too human confusion is the assurance that with further study will come order and beauty and a deeper understanding."

Jacob Bronowski

Protest and Prospect

41

Jacob Bronowski

Protest and Prospect

THE ESSAY THAT FOLLOWS is presented, as its title suggests, in two main parts. The first part, which consists of sections I to IV, is diagnostic, in that it analyzes the special character of the contemporary movements of protest, particularly in the universities. My conclusion is that the underlying motive for protest is not, as in the past, a wish to establish a planned and specific social organization different from the present one, but rather is a deep dissatisfaction with the aims and ethics of present society—a moral revulsion, not a political one.

At the end of the first part of the essay, I have interposed a short excursion in section V about the practical causes of unrest in the universities, which give a focus to these profound but generalized feelings of discontent. But the second part of the essay, in sections VI to IX, is of course concerned with a deeper, prescriptive question: how to recreate an ethic which shall give what we are all asking for, a sense of human purpose and social justice in one. Those who look back to the past (and they include some protesters) believe that the confidence in human

43

destiny which religion used to give has been eroded by science; and there is therefore a bias against science in their outlook. My view is the opposite; I think it is the failure to integrate into our culture the ethical and social implications of science that has undermined our own faith in ourselves. What I propose in the second part of the essay is therefore a natural philosophy of man, which has three constituents: a biological science of man, an anthropological science of society, and an immersion in the arts as a different expression of the nature of man. These seem to me to be the essential components of any culture (and any curriculum) that wants truly to be relevant to the life and condition of man in the twentieth century.

I

I must begin with a reminder that protest is not an invention of the 1960s—and this whether we think it a divine invention or a satanic one. On the contrary, protest has always been the normal apparatus by which to initiate change in human societies. Whenever we say of some historic pioneer that he was *original*, we imply that he was at odds with the traditional outlook of his day, and that he ultimately persuaded others to his view of things by voicing his dissent.

This is most obvious in the sciences which, from Galileo to Albert Einstein, have always had to question the established explanations and replace them with new ones. So one reason for the growth of heterodoxy has no doubt been the spread of scientific education. Yet the same march of innovation, the same process of dissent and challenge, is evident in other intellectual fields: for example, in the arts and in philosophy. It has been equally important in politics and social reform; there could have been no American Revolution and no French Revolution without such unorthodox men as Benjamin Franklin, Thomas Jefferson, and Voltaire.

Lest that remark be passed over lightly, I pause to recall that I am speaking as an Englishman to what King George III would have called a "parcel of rebels"— that is, an audience of Americans. You are a republic today because your forefathers were impatient of social wrongs, what they called "a long train of abuses and usurpations," and revolted against them in 1776. This country was made by political dissenters and, even before that, by religious dissenters. Unlike most of you, I am not a Christian either: so it is fair that I remind you that you would not be what you are if Christ had submitted to the religious authority of his elders—or if Luther had done so later. It is a sobering lesson in history that millions of people who dislike the contemporary forms of protest still call themselves *Protestants*, a word which commemorates a historic act of protest against religious and political discrimination in 1529.

Progress by dissent then is characteristic of human societies. It has been responsible for the growth and success of democracy in the last four hundred years, and the decline and failure of absolute forms of government. For the crucial feature of democracy is not simply that the majority rules, but that *the minority is free to persuade people* to come over to its side and make a new majority. Of course the minority is abused at first—Socrates was, and so was Charles Darwin. But the strength of democracy is that the dissident minority is not silenced; on the contrary, it is the business of the minority to convert the majority; and this is how a democratic society invigorates and renews itself in change as no totalitarian society can.

Finally, it is natural that all through history the protesters have belonged to the younger generation, and the defenders of tradition have been the older men. This is one reason why dissent has usually come from the centers of learning, and has often begun as an intellectual movement before becoming a popular one. It was so, for example, in the time of Erasmus, and again in the decades of ferment that preceded the Russian Revolution. There are several new factors that underline this tendency today, to which I shall point later.

II

We see in general that protest is the age-old instrument for human progress. Yet when this has been said to link past to present, it remains evident that there are also differences, and that protest today has some features which are special and contemporary.

One feature that is peculiar to North America is that the movement of dissent here is greatly occupied with getting justice and equality for racial minorities. I shall refer to this important aim again, but I shall not speak about it much, because I cannot do so at first hand. I am a newcomer to this continent; my experience is almost wholly in European universities; and I shall therefore concentrate on those aspects of student dissent which American universities share with European universities.

The striking and universal feature in the protest of the young all over the world is that *it is not doctrinal.* We have been accustomed in the past to associate new movements with some specific dogma: with women's suffrage, for instance, or socialism, or land reform, or even National Socialism. There are no such ideological cure-alls in the minds of students today. Certainly they dislike the existing organizations of government pressure and social conformity, and they want them replaced by something more egalitarian, more personal, less rigid and manipulating. But the very fact that the students' protest runs across the existing political boundaries, from Berkeley to Warsaw, and from Prague to Paris and London, shows that there is no ideology which they think will solve the problems of the world overnight. The young now do not expect to reform society by a ready-made program with the points numbered from 1 to 14.

In particular, it is wide of the mark to think that dissent in North America is inspired by communism. Most students now find that idea laughable; they consider communism in East Europe to be a mechanical and dictatorial system of state which is as repugnant to them as any other autocracy. Otherwise why would the universities in Poland have made their remarkable protests in 1968? The Polish establishment called those demonstrations a capitalist plot, of course, and that makes a neat match to the fears of our establishment. But the students in Poland and Czechoslovakia are not rooting for capitalism, and the students in the west are not rooting for communism: they are united in *rejecting both establishments.*

It is easy to be scornful of all this, and to say that the students' very lack of dogma proves that theirs is an impractical and romantic approach to changing the world. Indeed it is: the heroic pictures of Mao and of Che Guevara on the walls of dormitories show that. It may even be called negative and, worse, a purely destructive approach. But these easy criticisms miss what is crucial and new in the outlook of the young of today. They are

47

not merely criticizing the systems of state in which their elders live, either east or west of the Berlin wall. They are criticizing the *systems of values* by which their elders live everywhere.

So the students' protest is not doctrinal because it goes much deeper: it is concerned with ethics. In the past there was a simple difference between the generations, all the way from politics to sports: the old were usually in favor of the status quo and the young were usually in favor of change. But simple differences like these, simple labels like "conservative" and "liberal," will no longer do now. Now the difference between the generations is a total difference in posture—a rejection by each of the norms by which the other lives.

III

The generation gap is now a moral chasm, across which the young stare at their elders with distrust, convinced that the values that make for success are fake. Evidently the first field in which young people are struck by this suspicion is public life, and there the undeclared war in Vietnam has had a disastrous impact. Who indeed could have believed that, only twenty-five years after Pearl Harbor, national policy would be carried on like this?

Young people would like to be proud of their own nation (that, after all, is what the students from the minorities are doing) and they were shocked to find that they could not be proud of the policy of America and her allies in Asia. This was coupled with a second shock when they found that they could not be proud of the weapons and methods with which the war was waged.

But the greatest shock of all to the idealism of the young is the way in which official spokesmen manipulate and even hoodwink the public opinion that they are supposed to lead. A whole apparatus of evasion has been developed in which nothing is an outright lie, and yet nothing quite means what it seems to say. The very words are unreal: de-escalation, ultimate deterrent, agonizing reappraisal—a tasteless vocabulary of plastic which George Orwell prophetically called Newspeak.

Plainly this language is not designed to *state* a policy but to *sell* it, and accordingly it is tailored to each audience in turn: the patriots here, the realists there, and the credulous everywhere. No wonder that students on both sides of the Iron Curtain think that politics is a career for actors rather than principals. This state of affairs has become so notorious in some countries that it has been christened with an euphemism all of its own: it is called the credibility gap. That politely evasive phrase describes what is the fundamental outrage to democracy, namely the concealment of knowledge, and more than anything else, I believe, this has been responsible for sapping the trust of the young in public standards. We cannot present George Washington and Abraham Lincoln as heroes at school, and expect students to accept lower standards in high places when they get to college.

It would be comforting if we could stop there and say, yes, some men in high places have disappointed the young, but after all they have their parents and teachers to look up to still. Unhappily, it is just here that the generation gap is different now from what it was thirty years ago. I can speak for this from my own experience, and I will do so.

I was brought up in Europe in an orthodox Jewish household. My father was a devout believer, who was meticulous to the point of obsession in the practice of every detail of his religious faith. By the time that I went to college I no longer shared his beliefs, which seemed to me an anachronism. But I did not doubt for a moment that my father was sincere in what he believed and practiced. No one, not even the mutinous son that I was, could have thought my father a hypocrite. And as I respected him, so he respected me—in spite of my skepticism. My father thought me a hot-head, but he did not doubt that I was sincere too.

Today the generation gap cleaves through families and colleges, and there is little respect left in it. I need not trouble to spell out for you what the fathers think—and worse still, the grandfathers: they are the ones who write to the papers with such venom every day. Yet I must not quite neglect the phenomenon of those letters to the newspapers. Here we are in the country which prizes education more than any other country in the world; and in that country, I live in the state of California, which prizes education more than any other state. And yet exactly here the correspondence columns are filled with such hatred against the young, such hysterical fear of change, that one cannot imagine how the writers picture a university. Do they expect education to run backwards? Do they think that there can be progress without originality, and originality without dissent? Or would they really like to burn heretics?

Perhaps senior citizens always felt like this, and their grandsons paid no attention. But now the same gap has opened between fathers and sons. Whatever the generation, the sons no longer believe that the standards by which their elders judge them are genuine; on the contrary, they strike them for the most part as bald hypocrisy.

I knew that my father lived by the precepts which he tried to impose on me. But most students today are convinced that their parents and teachers deceive themselves and profess a traditional set of principles without even being aware that they do not live by them. In the eyes of the children, the generation gap now is a hypocrisy gap.

IV

If those whom the young stigmatize were all reactionaries and anti-intellectuals it would be easy to concur. Unfortunately things are not so simple. A whole generation of liberals and humanists, to which I belong, is bewildered at the discovery that the young include us in their charge of hypocrisy. We made liberalism respectable by our labors, and turned it into an intellectual faith; and now we are distressed to find that our heroic memories of the hungry thirties and the Spanish Civil War are dismissed as an out-of-date mythology.

The fact is that we, the generation of intellectuals, have been a success, and our liberal and even radical ideas have not stood in our way on the road to affluence. And the young are suspicious of affluence: they do not believe that success comes so cheap to those who hold their principles dear. Success is a commodity sold on television in shatter-proof bottles at bargain prices, and the children are no longer impressed by those trappings of authenticity. They know in their hearts that the successful man is a prisoner of the status quo, whatever high principles he may avow in the family circle or on the rostrum.

When the French historian La Popclinière died obscurely in 1608 his biographer wrote that he died "of a disease common to men of learning and virtue, that is, of misery and of want." But that was in the past. Now men of learning fare much better, and their sons and students are correspondingly less certain of their virtue.

So it is not to be wondered that the young are restive when they hear us pay lip-service to intellectual truth. For in the thirty years in which we have preached that, the world has changed, and we have somehow forgotten to find new foundations for the old truths. The economic exploitation and social inequality of thirty years ago have been transformed since then, and will no longer do as grounds for the human and liberal morality in which we still believe—and believe rightly. As intellectuals, we have done little to formulate afresh *an ethic of liberalism on foundations which are modern and valid now*. In my view, this is the central criticism that can be directed against intellectuals today, in and out of the universities.

V

Here I must pause in my argument to say something about the practical discontents in the universities. For of course there are direct and practical causes that turn the moral scruples of students into the bitter hand-to-hand clashes with campus authority. Three causes are specifically modern, and illustrate how the education of today differs from that of the past—even the past of thirty years ago.

First, there are vastly more students now than there have ever been before. There are about eight million of them in North America alone, at this moment—more than went to college in the whole world throughout all of the last century. What students in such vast numbers want from university education must be different in kind from the academic programs of the past. So we are now engaged by necessity in the experiment of finding a central core of knowledge and a culture to embody the aspirations of mass democracy. This is the cardinal problem to which I shall come in the second part of this essay. The demands of the minority groups for higher education are one part of the problem we have to solve. But the problem is the same for the majority, and is world-wide: what is the central content of contemporary knowledge that every young man and woman (and not just a few) ought to have in order to feel and act as educated citizens?

Second, young people now become physically and emotionally mature almost two years earlier than they did in the past. Yet while the age of biological maturity has fallen steadily, the age of university education has remained almost unchanged. As a result, the campuses are now peopled by grown men and women, yet are governed by traditions of organization and discipline which were made for adolescents. No wonder that parents who remember themselves as striplings at college are outraged by the beards and the bosoms that they see there now—and by the intransigence that is natural in the bearded and the bosomed, especially when they have to be treated as children. The university system as it is, historically, is two years out of step with the attitudes and emotions of contemporary students, and is only suited to the young who are now in high school.

And third, the trouble on campus is a microcosm that reflects the troubles of administration and organization that dog any mass democracy. I have already said that democracy is a very special philosophy. It expresses the mind of the majority, yet it gives the minority the right to try to change the mind of the majority. That is, democracy is an instrument for change and progress.

But to make that philosophy work, democracy has to have an administration which is receptive to change. It has to be sensitive to what people want *before* they break the rules. And this is where organizations of state and government are failing us all, and where, most seriously, the campus administrations are failing the students. I have been an administrator myself and I know the temptations. There is always some piece of business in the office which seems more urgent than the complaints of people. So the awkward issues are postponed; the grievances accumulate; and we stumble from crisis to crisis, never acting until the strike notices have been posted and people's blood is up. We never tackle a frontier dispute until there is shooting; a labor demand until the garbage is piled high in the streets; and the restlessness of the young until they invade the president's office.

The trouble on campus has a tremendous message: that we must discover how to run mass democracy so that things are changed *before* people get mad. In an age of technology, of constant practical change, this is a practical message to shake the world. Because if we do not get this right, then the process of peaceful change will break down and people will turn to violence and minority rule everywhere. The trouble on campus is a storm signal to warn us that the philosophy of democracy will only survive if we reform the *practice* of democracy.

VI

Yet when these practical things have been said, the intellectual problem comes back to meet us. We need to find a philosophical foundation for the ethics of democracy that the young can believe in. What divides democracy from its enemies is not a dogmatic distinction as between good and bad, your faith and mine, but it is the basic distinction between tolerance and fanaticism—between persuasion and violence. When the students turn to disruption and hooliganism they show that our generation has failed to make the liberal values real to them. Instead we have demonstrated to them in a dozen political precedents, all the way from Ireland to Israel, that only men with guns get their demands met. And calling out the National Guard will only reinforce that ugly lesson.

The young are looking for a universal ethic now as much as in the past, and here as much as in Czechoslovakia. If they strike you as amoral, look again: they are in search of a morality which shall be idealistic and realistic at the same time. And if we think we have it in humanism, we shall have to find modern foundations for that.

It is pointless to exhort students to "law and order," and to lecture them about "rights and duties," in the absence of any foundation for human respect—and worse, in an atmosphere of cynicism that claims that human nature is a caged beast. Law and order are not ends in themselves; they are means that society has invented to preserve *justice*, which is the harmony between individual freedom and communal need. Since only man among the animals is both individual and social, he has constantly to re-create the balance between these two sides of his nature. What we have to ask of people, then, young and old alike, is not that they respect the law blankly, but that they respect every man as a man, whatever his opinions or his social function. And to bring that about, we have to make a modern analysis of the nature of man, derived from the natural and social sciences and equally from its expression in the arts. Only thus shall we establish for everyone that the identity of man demands respect as an essential and, as it were, an existential condition of his being.

This is in a sense an academic program, and none the worse for that; and the universities are to be blamed for failing to attempt it. In a time of bold technical progress and of brilliant scientific discovery, one might have expected that humanists in the universities would also be eager to move into new fields, and that the study of the ethical nature of man would be most attractive to them. After all, many of the protesting students are suspicious of science and disillusioned by it, and are ready to look to the humanities for a lead. But in fact the departments of humanities have done little to move away from their traditional studies and toward the ethical content of their own subject matter. And yet that is surely what the arts can teach: the sense of identity with the inner lives of all men.

It is particularly sad that philosophy has remained remote from any genuine enquiry into the human mind and the dilemmas of personality. At a time when young men hunger for principles to guide their lives, philosophy has been preoccupied with forms of analysis in which, it righteously assures them, there surely are none to be found. So for thirty years now no philosopher has commanded, or has aspired to, that combination of intellectual and moral respect which made Bertrand Russell a giant in his generation.

VII

I believe that there are principles to be found today to guide human conduct as there were in the past. They must come out of modern knowledge of what makes us the creatures we are, specifically human. We do not know the whole answer to that, of course, and no doubt we never will; but we know more than we ever did in the past. And what we know is not exclusively in science, and not exclusively in the humanities, but is a combination of both in which each illuminates the other. Only in this way, by understanding as exactly and as sympathetically as we can what men are, can we make the generations (past and present) agree to try to be what men should be.

In my view, this is a very practical task: for an agreed ethic must be based on a common culture, and a common culture must be expressed in what is taught in schools and universities. The great need, the great experiment in education, therefore, is to put together a central core of personal knowledge for teachers and students, a natural philosophy of man whose parts truly represent the constituents of modern culture. I think there should be three parts: science, anthropology (as representative of social study), and literature.

In science, students need in the first place to learn enough physics, chemistry, and mathematics (including some statistics) to make a foundation for biology in its contemporary form. As soon as they have the foundation, they should go on to biology as the central science in the curriculum. The accent in biology should be on evolution: the evolution of life, of molecular structures and processes, of organs, of species and their behavior, and in the end of man. The purpose should be to build up a picture of man as he is by nature, within the order of nature: what I have called elsewhere "an understanding of the evolution and the place of man" as a single conception. I will go on to quote what I said there:

He is, like the other primates, noisy, inquisitive, cooperative, intelligent, skillful, thoughtful, and as busy with himself as with his environment. These features are not common in the rest of the animal world, singly or in combination. They have been a great deal more important in the evolution of the primates than the territorial imperative and the aggressive drives which we share with other animals.

Evidently this does not look like the physics and chemistry or even the biology that is taught in school and university laboratories today. But what makes it different has much more to do with the purpose of teaching science than with the content of what is taught. Good physicists, good chemists, and good professional biologists will be needed in the future as in the past—and needed not only for the practical progress of their subjects but for the most practical reason of all, which is the intellectual beauty of the subjects themselves as high points of human achievement. But the teaching of science to nonscientists has a different purpose, for which the professional and the specialist can supply no substitute: the purpose of making the physical world personal to each of us in our own abilities and experiences. Therefore science for nonscientists needs to be directed towards an understanding of nature as she expresses herself in us, the human creatures. We need to feel a personal pleasure in the way her machinery works, and above all in the very special gifts of coordination and knowledge which the machinery of nature has created in us. Let me continue my quotation:

> And in the remarkable order of primates, the evolution of man is most remarkable and spectacular. His gifts of discrimination and judgment, the ability to speak, to remember, to foresee, to imagine and to think symbolically, his

carriage and the freedom that it gives to hands and face, his face-to-face relations and his way of making love, his family life and the intimacy of his social values, are an incomparable biological equipment. They have evolved him, and in turn have been evolved by his own progress, within at most a few million years. From them he has his creative skill and his imaginative breadth of outlook, in which are intertwined his need for the society of others and his urge to think for himself.

VIII

As the second leg in what I call my tripos curriculum I have chosen anthropology. I prefer it to other branches of social study because I think students should not be preoccupied only with the forms of social institutions (including government) but should unravel the underlying beliefs and values which those express. Anthropology is the best discipline for the study of values, not as arbitrary social norms but as expressions of human aims.

It seems to me important in particular that we make it clear to ourselves (and to our students) that culture is as much a part of man's equipment as his opposable thumb and visual acuity are. Indeed it was the cultural use of these biological gifts that gave them a selective advantage and thereby accelerated their biological evolution in man. The capacity for culture is a human universal. Moreover, there are universals in all cultures, some of which are so difficult to explain (the prohibition of incest, for example) that they must be of unusual importance to the species. Thus the comparison between cultures, both when they are alike and when they differ, is a major intellectual requirement in the twentieth century. In this sense, anthropology carries on the scientific purpose of my first leg, and I can go on with my quotation for one step more:

> It goes without saying that the picture of man that science presents to a bewildered and downcast public must be truthful. But that does not mean that it turns him either into a beast or into a computer. On the contrary, what makes the biological machinery of man so powerful is that it modifies his actions through his imagination: it makes him able to symbolize, to project himself into the consequences of his acts, to conceptualize his plans, and to weigh them one against another as a system of values. We are the creatures who have to create values in order to elucidate our own conduct and to learn from it so that we can direct it into the future.

IX

For the third leg of my tripos I propose one of the dramatic arts: the drama itself, or literature extended to include the novel as well, or the cinema, which is the modern form of the drama. The choice among these arts is not crucial, but the presence in the curriculum of at least one of them is. If I have to make my own choice, then I propose literature, for two good reasons: that language is the single most important human gift, and that there is a long tradition of literature which joins us to other cultures. But I would not find fault with those who feel that the cinema, for example, has the advantage of spanning several arts, and of putting the spectator inside the skin of the actor in a way that is more immediate and powerful than any other. What the arts have to say to us, face to face, is not the monopoly of one of them.

The arts are important in the curriculum because they *express* the human condition directly, and as cogently as the sciences *expound* it. Literature in particular should give the student a sense of kinship in human problems, an open door into the minds and passions of men, within which he finds himself to be both singular and universal. The gift of imagination makes man able to live his own life and a thousand others, and to draw from that network of experience a central concept of himself that is not as commonplace as that presented to him by parents and preachers.

The business of the work of dramatic art (in which I include the novel and the film) is to make the spectator a participant. But that requirement, though it is right as far as it goes, does not go far enough; for example, it does not divide the good work of art from the bad—which is a crucial difference that we are conscious of even in the act of luxuriating in the bad. For the point is that the bad work *is* a luxury; it encourages the reader or the spectator to identify himself with trivial forms of success which we know to be unworthy even as we enjoy imagining ourselves in them. What else makes the appeal of the films about the jet set, the fantasies of sex in the paperbacks, the stories of gangsters and detectives and boxing champions, and the heart-rending death of the prison chaplain in the jail break?

These are the hopelessly unreal visions of wish-fulfillment that bad art sells us, to give us a hazy sense of well-being like alcohol. By contrast, good art is real because it makes us look into those parts of the human heart that we hide from ourselves. We share and feel the greed of the miser in Balzac, the emotion of the murderer in Dostoevski, the rages and frustrations and the lusts of the lynch mob in William Faulkner. And these are the passions that we abhor in others because we dare not acknowledge

61

them in ourselves. The great work of art acts on us like *Othello*, and makes us aware how pitiful, how foolish, and how natural are all the contrivances of that plot, from the black husband to the spotted handkerchief. And when we confess this to ourselves, when we understand that each of us is Othello and Desdemona, yes, and Iago too— then we understand the drama and ourselves in a single act. This is a mode of knowledge by inner experiences that no textbook can imitate, and it can be a better guide to conduct than any book of moral precepts. Since I have presented these views in *The Identity of Man,* I need not argue them here. I think they leave no doubt that literature can be as important a constituent in founding a modern ethic as can the sciences of biology and anthropology.

The need for a modern ethic of this kind, securely founded, is patent; precisely the lack of it has turned the movements of protest towards self-righteousness and violence. Otherwise we are simply on the way to confronting dogma with dogma, force with ferocity, my right with your wrong. But these do not constitute the real division in human conduct. The fundamental distinction is between liberal and bigot, and at bottom it is the distinction between human and inhuman. At the base of any educational reform, this is the distinction for which we have to find a secure, contemporary, and universal foundation.

Howard Mumford Jones

Scholarship and Relevance

Howard Mumford Jones' article, "Scholarship and Relevance," previously appeared in a 1970 issue of *The Southern Humanities Review*, by permission of The University of Alabama Press; the article has been revised for inclusion in the present volume.

Howard Mumford Jones

Scholarship and Relevance

I AM HONORED to be included in this series of lectures at Auburn University, the purpose of which everybody seriously interested in higher education in the United States must heartily applaud. Universities exist, or so it seems to me, as citadels of rationality, centers of intellectual order, places where the dispassionate examination of human life and human culture may be carried on with as little interference as possible from outside propagandists. Such at least is the concept towards which the American university struggled until after World War II, and hitherto this ideal has been acceptable to thoughtful citizens of all ages. I think it is still the right concept. The decline and fall of universities that have been captured by propaganda, or by an ideology, or by a political party, or by some popular anti-intellectual force indicate to me that when universities are forced into a mold alien to their purpose, the results are disastrous. Where for example, are either the great universities that were once among the glories of the Spanish Empire or those that nourished the splendid culture of the Saracens?

But the proper concept of a university is now attacked by a variety of forces—the intrusion of government into research; an alliance, sometimes beneficial, sometimes not, between the university and heavy industry; an impatient demand that our universities should immediately solve the complex social, political, and economic problems of our day; and a powerful, if hazy, rebellion among many students against the faculty, the rules, the courses, the grade system, the requirements, and the administration of these institutions. Of course student riots are nothing new in American educational history. In the second quarter of the nineteenth century Harvard undergraduates wrecked the college chapel because President Josiah Quincy had called in the police to put down student disorder; and Mr. Jefferson's University of Virginia in the same period was, I fear, as notable for student misconduct as it was for intellectual eminence. But the disturbances of today seem to exhibit a special quality that sets them apart from undergraduate rebellions in the past. I suppose the key word to this quality is "relevance".

Relevance is difficult to define. We have sent men to the moon at a cost of a good many billion dollars, an expenditure that did nothing relevant to slum clearance, peace in Vietnam, Black power, or the problem of the aged; yet the Americans, including battalions of the younger generation, assembled by thousands to express their joy in a technological rather than a humanitarian triumph. If you are opposed to the arms race, it is clearly relevant to protest against the misuse of engineering and chemical know-how for an over-kill. On the other hand the Americans have never been prepared for a major war; after Pearl Harbor it was nip-and-tuck whether we would survive; and history being a one-way process, experts cannot agree whether the atom bomb saved more lives than it destroyed or destroyed more lives than it saved. Is one to curtail departments of chemistry because napalm is a chemical invention? Who is to do the curtailing, and where are we to draw the line? Greek fire, in its day a secret chemical weapon of Byzantium, was a principal defense for an extraordinary empire which survived for a thousand years, shielded the West against pillage, and preserved, however imperfectly, the wisdom of the ancient world. The social sciences have always been divided between those who think their main purpose should be dispassionate analysis of problems and those who think economic and sociological expertise should immediately set to work for the improvement of mankind. Some student radicals, however, feel that unless universities are turned at once into reformatory schools of their liking, universities should be destroyed. But how do you know a practical pattern of reform unless you operate on some knowledgeable principle and not from emotionalism only? Emotionalism is not a program, as the leaders of the French revolution eventually found out. Religion and philosophy teach us to love our fellow men; but what if a considerable group of our fellow men not only fails to love us but distrusts us and seeks to destroy us? Recent troubles in Ulster show how vehemence and violence incite counter-violence and counter-vehemence, so that it would seem that one must recur to *some* rule of reason, some principle of tolerance and firmness. The university is a place for the analysis of problems; it cannot simultaneously be both partisan and non-partisan, it is neither a bandstand nor an arena but, quite properly, an academic island of calm midmost the beating of the steely sea.

67

My competency lies elsewhere than in political science, engineering, the sciences, and social studies. I turn therefore to the areas of history and the humanities and inquire what relevance means in these related studies.

Let me examine the simplest possible connotation of relevance; namely, the doctrine that only contemporary, or mainly contemporary, writers help us with present problems. Contemporary man should be guided by contemporary analyses. No proposition seems more plausible. Who else save the living shall interpret for us the troubles of our proud and angry time? The dead cannot do so. Moreover the most elementary knowledge of great figures in the literary past—(I stick to English literature)—shows that the majority of these gifted men were sensitive to injustice in their time. Why should our writers have lost this traditional sensitivity? If Shelley cried out against tyranny, why should not Cleaver have an equal right to do so? Living writers are living; Milton and Pope, Ben Johnson and Chaucer are both dead and remote.

This idea is supported by the precedent of almost any other political or literary era. Thus in the Tudor and Stuart periods an overwhelming problem was the power of the ruler, and from Bishop Bale's *King John* through most of Shakespeare's plays down through the dramas of Dryden and beyond, this theme is again and again discussed. A central topic in the Age of the Enlightenment was the mores of the middle class. Periodicals like the *Tatler* and the *Spectator*, poets, among them Thomas Gray and Edward Young, and novelists such as Richardson and Fielding took up the subject. In the next age, Burns, Blake, Byron, Wordsworth, Burke, Hazlitt, Coleridge, and a score of others were immensely stirred by the American and French revolutions, the Napoleonic wars, the social maladjustments of the industrial revolution, propaganda for the rights of women, the abolition of slavery, and the broadening of the suffrage. It is true these worthies did not come up with identical solutions, but they discussed the questions of their time, the balance of right and wrong, tradition and modernity (contrast Scott and Jeremy Bentham), conservatism and change. If you took away then current issues from Emerson, Thoreau, Hawthorne, Melville, William Gilmore Simms, Whittier and the rest, how much poorer our literature would be! Is it not, then, to retreat into that mythical edifice, the ivory tower, to assert or assume that our writers are not mirrors of our time? Of course, William Gilmore Simms and John Greenleaf Whittier did not see eye to eye in the matter of slavery, and Hawthorne's view of original sin was not shared by Walt Whitman, but they were all wrestling with current themes.

The rebel can, then, make an excellent case. The time is now, the struggle is here, and the strife of contending forces a thousand years hence or a thousand years ago does not concern him. Moreover, the establishments against which he rebels—the defense establishment, the university establishment, the police establishment, the judiciary establishment—are products of history, are embedded in history, are so governed by history, by precedent and rule, custom and tradition, the only way out is to smash the power of the past. As a country we are disinclined to recognize much wisdom in the old. As a culture we have some difficulty in giving thought to posterity; witness the struggles of a small minority to preserve air, water, and soil from pollution, the incessant battle of a few conservationists to hold on to some parts of our dwindling landscape beauty. Our advertising perpetually appeals to today and to tomorrow; our religion abandons inherited wickedness, transforms sin, which is a theological concept, into guilt, which is a psychiatric one, and purposes to find joy not in heaven but immediately on earth. The battle of the generations was well put by an American poet:

> Said the old men to the young men,
>   "Who will take arms to be free?"
>
> Said the young men to the old men,
>   "We."
>
> Said the old men to the young men,
>   "It is finished. You may go."
>
> Said the young men to the old men,
>   "No."
>
> Said the old men to the young men,
>   "What is there left to do?"
>
> Said the young men to the old men,
>   "You."

I hope the fact that this bit of verse was written about half a century ago by Wytter Binner will not trouble you. Even the most radical youth may generously admit that an elder generation had some dim gleam of truth; otherwise they would not appeal to Karl Marx, who is dead, nor chant the slogans of Chairman Mao, who is an old man.

The grip of contemporaneousness on our civilization is clearly not a monopoly of people under thirty. Our technological culture lives in a perpetual present tense. In science the past is mostly a tissue of errors it is the purpose of research to eradicate and advance beyond: for-

70

merly the Ptolemaic system, then the universe of Newton, now the enigmatic cosmos of Einstein; formerly the doctrine of final causes, then the universality of cause and effect, now the theory of statistical probability. The screw of Archimedes was in its day a dazzling creation, but we are living in the age of electronics and atomic energy. Despite charges of irrelevance against social science courses, the principal concern of those disciplines is with present problems in an era when Keynesian economics is old hat, and computerized demographic tables are somehow to save us all. Even the contemporary vogue of archaeology seems as much motivated by the desire to illumine present art and custom as by dispassionate curiosity about empires that have vanished; and we appear to study anthropology for the light totem and tabu may cast upon puberty, psychiatry, matriarchal tyranny, drug-taking, and religion now.

Despite the excellence of historians, our educational systems, our religions, our values, our advertising, and our costumes are probably less influenced by history today than were these same aspects of life in the New World in any major period of the past. True, we preserve Williamsburg and Old Sturbridge, Ford's Theater and General Lee's horse, Mount Vernon and Spanish missions in the Southwest, but we preserve them as museum pieces, not as symbols of virtue and wisdom; and it is characteristic, I think, that, first the Fourth-of-July oration; second, the famous phrase, "a gentleman of the old school"; and third, the political theory of a representative republic (for which we substitute the word "democracy") have vanished from public discourse and private conversation. Yet in this fashion of unhistorical thought we have, whether we know it or not, returned in fact upon history and repeated it. What we have accepted is an ancient concept of temporality. *We* are not as modern as *we* think *we* are; *we* are merely medieval.

To medieval man history did not exist except as lapse of time between Creation and the Day of Judgment. He thought of human life therefore in a perpetual present tense. The Greeks in Chaucer's *Troilus and Cressida* are knights and ladies of the age of chivalry, and the histories of Orosius, who wrote about the universe, and of the Venerable Bede, who wrote about England, are mere chronicles—calendars that repeat the years and the seasons, accounts of moral episodes illustrating providence and the saintliness or the depravity of man. Time did not stand still, of course; it revolved like the wheel on which the figure of Fortune stands in a thousand representations, the best known of which is the engraving by Albrecht Dürer. Time was repetition, not change; circular, never parabolic. In habits, thought, motive, and speech Charlemagne, Aeneas, Isold, Mohammed, Helen of Troy, Constantine the Great, and Frederick Barbarossa were all contemporaries wearing the same costumes. Dante possessed a considerable reading knowledge of the past, but in the *Divine Comedy* saints, sinners, pagans, and a few virtuous heathen are assigned their places in hell, purgatory, and paradise as they succumbed to the endless temptations of Satan or represented the eternal goodness of God yesterday, today, and forever.

Cardinal Newman once distinguished between notional assent and real assent. Notional assent is the acceptance we yield to the proposition that the square on the hypotenuse of a right-angled triangle is equal to the sum of the squares on the other sides. This is true, but nobody has gone to the barricades to defend it. Real assent, however, is deep, unswerving emotional allegiance, the kind of assent that the SDS, or the Communist Party, or the Black Panthers, or the John Birch Society, or Jehovah's Witnesses, or devout Catholics yield to tenets that seem to them so extremely true they admit of neither argument nor contradiction. The proposition that the American establishment, rotten to the core, must be destroyed; the proposition that a cynical government led us into the Vietnam war from sinister motives; the proposition that freedom demands the utmost liberty in speech and conduct if the creative life is not to be damaged; the proposition that anarchy is better than capitalism; the proposition that university trustees, administrators, and most professors are in a tacit conspiracy to repress dissent, ignore students, and maintain the military establishment —propositions of this kind demand of all true believers real, not notional, assent. But the proposition that man, ninety-nine percent of whose existence has been spent in the paleolithic age, improves painfully and slowly; the proposition that contemplation and analysis may be necessary counterweights to activism; the proposition that emotionalism needs to be channeled through critical intelligence; the proposition that Jane Austen probably knew as much about the female sex as the author of *Lolita*; the proposition that St. Augustine experienced as troublesome a spiritual malaise as did Hart Crane; the proposition that Balzac understood a society dedicated to making profits better than Saul Bellow understands it; the proposition that the triumph and tragedy of Julius Caesar may throw light on the triumph and tragedy of World War II—to propositions of this sort our schools, our colleges, our students, and our teachers seem to give only notional assent, if, indeed, they give any assent whatsoever.

But the duty of the university is not to put up with real assent and not be content with notional assent but to strike somewhere in between: to make it clear, for example, that there was wisdom in the world before President John F. Kennedy and folly in a world in which slogans and violence are supposed to be proper to educated men.

I have, however, strayed from an examination of the idea that living artists mirror the age in which they live; that, in a famous figure of speech, the writer is a mirror moving down the roadway and reflecting whatever is there. When one begins to think about the vogue of present slogans, the book of today, the drama of the immediate, and the poetry of tomorrow, and of equivalent manifestations in other arts from rock-and-roll to sculpture assembled from an automobile graveyard, one confronts a difficult question. Is the living writer, thinker, composer, painter, or whatever, representative of the totality of our culture, its whole conscience, its general wickedness, its social or philosophic aims; or does he represent only some part of that society in the sense that Burke represented conservatism, Tom Paine represented radicalism, and William Wordsworth moved along a line that ran from radicalism to reaction in their time?

Well, the first question concerns the status of an artist —say, a writer—in any society. At one period the poet was a member of the priestly caste, supposed to have special access to deity and to know the rites of the tribe. In a later phase he was a combination of historian and bard, as in the instance of Homer. In another time he was the embodiment of philosophical detachment and commentary, expressing truths beyond the capacity of ordinary men; such was the poet according to Plato and such were mystics like St. John of the Cross, William Blake; and our own Emerson. Another function was that of censor: he adopted as his norm inherited patterns of conduct because experience had proved their survival value, and he condemned deviations from these by ridiculing those who deviated. Such were Aristophanes, Horace, the Restoration dramatists, Alexander Pope, and e.e. cummings. After the Industrial Revolution, when fiction became the predominant form of writing, and literature depended upon commerce rather than patronage for its support, the author was pulled two ways. On the one hand he could be, in a favorable sense, an artist fashioning words into beautiful form, as did Flaubert and Walter Pater; on the other he became an entertainer selling his wares to the public. In this capacity he might be a literary hack like the makers of wild west stories; or he might rise to the level of a Scott, Balzac, or Trollope. If he did, he exhibited the qualities one associates with the higher imagination, as in the character creations of George Eliot or the compassion and terror one finds in novels by Dostoevski or Tolstoi, or in a book like Hemingway's *The Old Man and The Sea.*

Throughout these transformations the writer retained a sense of being set apart, a reputation for queerness and insight, a belief that he was not as other men, so that society was indulgent to his foibles and his temperament. But this meant of course that he belonged to a special class of men and had a special point of view with all its virtues and its limitations. The schools recognize this truth. They create a post for him called the writer in residence, as they do not create a post called the scientist in residence or the sociologist in residence. They devise special training courses for him, in which, at a low level, he may master a craft as a plumber does, and at a higher level learn to shape whatever talent or genius compels him to say. This shaping implies form. Form, it is clear, prejudices reflection; that is, form is not a mere reflection of experience, just as it is not a case study, but an interpretative surrogate for report. The conventions of form, though they alter from age to age, mix imagination with actuality. Form is indeed elemental, even in the case of *Tristram Shandy* or James Joyce. I recall a wise saying of T.S. Eliot that the spirit killeth, the letter maketh alive, by which he meant that undisciplined outpouring is futile because mere verbal anarchy cannot communicate pity, terror, comprehension, or humor. Form circumscribes, but formlessness is not a better guarantee of truth.

The theory that the contemporary writer directly reflects society—that he is, in that famous figure, a mirror moving down the road—is open, it seems to me, to this fundamental correction. Even though he be a realist, the writer is by nature and nurture neither a businessman nor a laborer, a clubwoman nor a prostitute; but somebody set apart by talent or genius who impresses shape on whatever he writes. But shaping words is no passive imitation of factuality. A generalization such as that the poor ye have always with you, or that the wise vendor buys in the cheapest market and sells in the dearest, is one thing; a book like Nelson Algren's *The Man with the Golden Arm* is something quite different. A poem, a novel, a play must have structure, and structure means that you alter what you see, choosing this, refusing that, adding emotional value to this event, hurrying over that one, refusing this apparent motive and emphasizing some other. The writer is neither a police sergeant nor a social worker. If one denies that Dickens's *Dombey and Son* is an objective record of the London business world of the 1840's, which clearly it is not, one must also question whether Mr. Algren's novel, however moving, reflects the totality of life even on Skid Row in Chicago. If one says that the autobiographical formula of *Huckleberry Finn* imposes a certain contrivance on Mark Twain, it is fair inference that the pseudobiographical formula of Philip Roth's *Portnoy's Complaint* likewise implies contrivance on this author's part. Perhaps the point is obvious. But since productions like the Roth novel, certain late or current theatrical successes, and the poetry published in *The Evergreen Review* are said to reflect a sick society, scholarship is bound to inquire how far literature really reflects society, sick or well.

Not only do form and the temperament of the artist intervene, but every age has its fashion in style or form; as, the Gothic novel, Euphuism, the heroic couplet, and the conventions of courtly love. A future age will probably find our Freudian fiction as artificial as we find the Gothic novel. What then becomes of our mirror?

Let me transfer the problem of the trustworthiness of literature as immediate report to a more distant time. I select the eighteenth century, the Age of Enlightenment, and I begin with Thomas Paine, possibly the most influential propagandist in American literary history. How far does he reflect his own era? His pamphlets, *Common Sense* and the *Crisis* series, are fundamental to any study of the American Revolution. His *The Rights of Man* was the most effective answer to Edmund Burke, and his *The Age of Reason* has merit as a popular statement of deism, a demagogic attack on Christianity, and a denunciation of theology, the church, and the English Bible. He was a master of pungent prose. His biographer asserts, I know not on what evidence, that *Common Sense* sold half a million copies in a country of three million, and it seems to be true that 120,000 copies were sold in the first three months after printing. He has been called the Morning Star of the Revolution, as well as other things less flattering. This certainly looks like "relevance." Did Paine mirror American society from 1776, when *Common Sense* appeared, to 1787, when he went to England?

In the first place, though Paine was secretary to the foreign affairs committee of the Continental Congress and at one time served as clerk of the Pennsylvania Assembly, he knew nothing at first hand of the colonies outside eastern Pennsylvania, northern New Jersey, and the environs of New York City. In the second place, of his seventy-two years, he spent only twenty in the New World, and of these twenty the last seven were spent in a cloud of obloquy because the country as a whole had repudiated his religious opinions. Of the thirteen years between 1774 and 1787, the last six he lived in semi-retirement; having been found guilty of indiscretions, he lost his congressional post after only two years of service. It appears, first, that he knew only a small portion of American life; second, that not all Americans trusted him; and third, that however brilliant his style and sincere his devotion to liberty, no historian accepts his characterization of George III, of monarchy, of the church, of Jewish history, or of American opinion. Moreover, only about a third of the colonists actively supported revolution, nor did all of the third feel that Paine expressed their opinions. One admires him as a stylist, but as a mirror moving down the roadway and reflecting what it sees, Paine is a distorting mirror.

Let me go on to the Age of the Enlightenment in general. One admirable book, *The Age of Ideas*, by George R. Havens declares that there then arose in France a corps of brilliant writers, leaders of thought and masters of style, whose books, though banned by the censor, were widely read by what he calls the general public. Peter Gay's *The Enlightenment* speaks of that movement as a single army with a single banner, a large central body, a right and left wing, daring scouts, and lame stragglers, and affirms that proponents of the Enlightenment shared a common experience and a common philosophy. In an excellent study, *The Age of the Enlightenment*, Sir Isaiah Berlin calls the eighteenth century the last age in Western Europe when human omniscience was thought obtainable, admires the intellectual power, honesty, lucidity, courage, and love of truth among its gifted proponents, and says the period is one of the most hopeful in the history of man. Surely here is scholarly testimony to show that literature reflects the problems of its time.

I admire these studies but I question some of their generalizations. What was the "general public" the scholars refer to? In the first place, though we have no good statistics for the Atlantic community, we know that the mass of people in the eighteenth century simply could not read. In the next place, of the literate minority only a minority accepted the radicals as mirrors of their time. Conservatives like Burke, Joseph de Maistre, and Genz repudiated them, and a prudent middle class went only part way with them. Thousands of Christians abhorred "infidels" like Voltaire, Holbach, and Tom Paine. Another powerful literate group—employers, bankers, army officers, landlords, clergymen, court officials, judges—did not care for dangerous ideas. Moreover, if scholars stress the affirm-

79

ative aspect of the Enlightenment, other eighteenth-century men, if they accepted rationalism at all, drew from it cynical, sceptical, antagonistic, or pessimistic inferences; for example, Jonathan Swift, Dr. Johnson, John Adams, Rousseau, Frederick the Great, and Edward Gibbon. Finally, the eighteenth-century world, even among the cultivated, was by no means wholly committed to rationalism, since the era was also the age of pietism, quietism, Wesleyanism, mysticism, the cult of sensibility, the cult of the beautiful soul, and of sentimental interpretations of God, nature, domesticity, childhood, and death, not to speak of the vogue of the Gothic north, primitivism, the noble savage, illuminism, uneducated poets, and a repudiation of reason as a false or diabolical guide. If one admires Locke, Berkeley, and Hume, Montesquieu, Beccaria, Condorcet, and others, one must also remember that no century excelled the Enlightenment in producing quackery and flimflam. Examples include John Law's Mississippi Bubble, the South Sea Bubble, tulipomania, Cagliostro, Mesmer, Joanna Southcote (who was going to give birth to the Messiah but failed to do so), Casanova and his cabalism, the many entries under "Ghosts" in Boswell's Johnson, the faked poems of Ossian and Chatterton, and Dr. Perkins's metallic tractors—metal rods that, used to stroke a patient, conveyed a mystical healing power to all his nerves and muscles.

Which of these varying groups, if any, reflects the problems of the eighteenth century? If we choose one, we shall have to minimize or ignore the others; yet the persons we discard in all probability thought they were intimate with the problems of their age. If we say that all of the writers mentioned reflect some of the problems of the time, we are undoubtedly correct—and we are faced with certain apparent contradictions. There were persons then—for example, Rousseau—who said that society was sick; there were other persons—for example, Condorcet—who thought that society must inevitably and forever progress; and there were still other persons —for example, John Adams—who thought that the lot of man did not differ greatly from one century to another. Which is the truer mirror of a young man's life, the Roderick Random of Tobias Smollet, the Tom Jones of Henry Fielding, or the extremely damp hero of Henry Mackenzie's once popular *The Man of Feeling?* Why do we turn up our noses at *The Vicar of Wakefield* as a picture of family life, and accept without cavil the family life of Clarissa Harlowe? Who or what truly mirrors the sexuality of the century—Fanny Hill, the eminently virtuous Pamela, the flirtatious Manon Lescaut, Charlotte of Goethe's *Sorrows of Young Werther,* the women who popped in and out of bed with Casanova, or the pornographic verse of Robert Burns? Which was the true guide to male conduct, Steele's *The Christian Hero* or Lord Chesterfield's *Letters to My Son?* Is the representative ruler George Washington or Frederick the Great? Once we get out from under the passions of our time and look at our problem in a context that cannot create prejudice, we see that contemporary writers then and contemporary writers now mirror only so much of life as interests them, and even that mirror is a distorting mirror.

Now that I have become involved with the eighteenth century, let me continue with it for a moment more. The so-called enlightened despots tried to modernize their governments. There occurred something called the Agricultural Revolution and something called the Industrial Revolution. It was the century of the American Revolution, the French Revolution, and spontaneous or contrived revolutions, abortive or successful, in the whole of the Western world. The curious thing about these revolutions is that most of their proponents appealed to history. The Agricultural Revolution was intended to carry out efficiently the wish of God, expressed in an old Hebrew book, that man should enjoy the fruits of the earth abundantly. The Industrial Revolution resulted from the application of science to labor; eighteenth-century scientists, like scientists later, thought they could depend upon the uniform operations of the universe as outlined by Sir Isaac Newton and felt, as the phrase then went, that they were only thinking God's thoughts after him. The leaders of the American Revolution appealed to precedent —to the government of ancient Israel, to the constitutions of the Greek and Roman republics, to the political practices of Renaissance Italy, to theorists of seventeenth-century England, and to the history of republican states like Geneva. The leaders of the French Revolution—a mixed bag, but I shall risk the simplification—sought to reinstitute the ancient customs of France, out of which came the idea of a meeting of the States General would save the nation; and when that didn't work, they appealed to Greece and Rome, establishing a "republic," a word from the Latin, adopting the term "citizen," another such a word, wearing the liberty cap, which comes from ancient Phrygia, at one time or another setting up tribunes, consuls, dictators, a Council of Ancients and a Council of Five Hundred on the model of the Greeks, and ending with an "emperor," who regarded himself as the heir of Charlemagne and Augustus Caesar and tried to give imperial France the pomp and circumstance of imperial Rome.

At this point you may well feel bewilderment. Am I saying that leaders of these revolutions looked around in history books for justificatory precedents? Or am I saying all literature is distortion? Or am I arguing that marching backward in time to the glory that was Greece and the grandeur that was Rome is something to be recommended? Am I not suppressing the fact that there were genuine evils in France and lesser ones in America? Do I not realize that primitive agriculture was wasteful, that the Industrial Revolution, though it entailed a vast amount of greed and misery, in the long run improved the general condition of mankind?

There is force in these objections, but unfortunately too many read history or interpret scholarship in just this way. Ardent progressives and some demagogues down-grade history because they agree with Napoleon that it is a fable agreed on and with Henry Ford that it is bunk. The fashion of modern interpretation in the arts unfortunately approaches this point of view. Freudian criticism, for example, transfers backward modern theories of *Angst*, eroticism, and repression, emphasizing the importance of the *Oedipus Rex* of Sophocles and ignoring its serene sequel, *Oedipus at Colonus*. The modern producer makes a great to-do about staging *Troilus and Cressida* but rarely puts on the pastoral idyll *As You Like It*. John Donne, if we are to believe our contemporaries, is "modern"; John Dryden, a great artist and a great critic, is not. Amid his flashy Byronical rhetoric Melville had a tragic vision; Longfellow, who strove for a vision of peace, which we all desire, doesn't come off. We are all for Henry Adams; we are all against Macaulay. So far has this obsessive reading of the past in terms of the present tense infected our intelligence that a show of nineteenth-century painters held in Minneapolis this summer drew John Canady, the *New York Times* critic, almost half across the continent to discover there were geniuses in pigment before the Impressionists; and it took him three successive essays in the Sunday *Times* to express his astonishment and pleasure. Everybody knows, or thinks he knows, about Machiavelli; ask the next ten persons you meet when Alexander the Great lived and died and what was his contribution to civilization. Charles Dickens was a great comic writer; critics have turned him into a sort of Victorian Kafka. I am myself becoming uncertain whether Mark Twain or James Joyce wrote *The Adventures of Huckleberry Finn.*

I now inject into this discussion two commonplaces about scholarship. The first is that every age rewrites history to suit itself. The other is Emerson's injunction to read every writing in the light of the circumstances that brought it forth.

The rewriting of history is commonplace enough, and historians have not only given up hope that history can recover events as they actually occur but have also, in the last half century, produced quite an extraordinary library on the nature of historical truth, the possibility of getting at it, and the puzzle of knowing how you know when you arrive where you are going. It is also true that Shakespeare meant one thing in his own times, another in the Restoration, a third to Dr. Johnson's circle, a fourth to romantic critics like Schlegel and Coleridge, a fifth to the Victorians, and something else to us moderns. There may be fixed stars in the heaven of thought, but our spectrum analysis of what they radiate seems to differ from century to century. It is, however, one thing to admit fallibility in scholarship and another thing to deny its validity altogether.

The other horn of the dilemma is to deny the possibility of knowing anything with certainty, a philosophical assumption that runs through the ages. But this does not help the moderns. If cultures in the past produced erroneous judgment there is no apparent reason to suppose that our own age, the heir of all these wrongheaded centuries, has somehow stumbled upon infallible truth, and there is ample reason to suppose that we are very much like our ancestors. Of course one may say that as between error in the past and error today, one prefers living error, but this is not seriously asserted, and if it were, it would scarcely guarantee any notable lasting value to either revolution or reform. Indeed, given the rather unoriginal truth that all men are mortal, I think I would rather err with Socrates than Marshall McLuhan.

But the question is not whether scholarship is infallible, and traditional masterpieces never to be equalled; the question is what scholarship and masterpieces have to offer this or any other time. I suggest their lasting usefulness is that they correct modern impatience by inculcating the long-range view. By the long-range view I mean not only curbing our emotional impatience to get things done this month, I mean the possibility first, that when we recognize we are but one in a long succession of the generations of men, we shall not fall into the error of a verse in the Book of Job: "Doubtless ye are the people and wisdom will die with you"; and second, the useful truth that the successes and failures of the past may tell us something about the responsibilities of the state, the place of religion in many lands and centuries, the relative importance of various human characteristics, what happens to countries that have wasted their natural resources and denuded the soil and what happens in countries that have not, the long-run result of revolutions, the lasting satisfactions of life rather than the ephemeral ones. There may or may not be law in history, but there are certainly illuminating examples.

The second branch of my argument is that studying cultures totally different from ours—and here, I think, the moderns perform better than they do in other things —may tell us something about the solid satisfactions of life in value patterns alien to our own. I am incurably a moralist; and I hold in a special sense to the old-fashioned doctrine that scholarship has something to do with history teaching by example. Anybody who has visited Israel and seen what reforestation has done on one side of the Jordan River and what the failure to reforest has failed to do or succeeded in doing on the other side will have a striking lesson in what can be learned by comparing cultures.

One cannot foresee how the future historian of our time will label this age, but I should not be astonished if he called it the Era of Impatience. Patience is not an exciting virtue. It is also perfectly true that in the past a plea for patience has too often been a mask for inactivity or reaction. Patience will never satisfy the radical or the reformer, and I have small hope that my doctrine that the virtue of scholarship is the inculcation of a long-range view will persuade many. I, too, am conscious of a certain hollowness in adages like: "Rome was not built in a day" or "Heaven is not reached by a single bound." Nevertheless, the scientist develops patience, the surgeon develops patience, the psychiatrist develops patience, and so do the housewife, the farmer, the lawyer, and the scholar. America has produced few saints, and among these few none, I think, notably distinguished for the contemplative life, yet it is just possible that what we need is more patience rather than more reckless activity.

Relevance lies in the imagination of men. It is a linking together of whatever nourishes and fortifies the spirit, and I have tried to indicate, however imperfectly, that the history of humanity may fortify, and should not imprison, the going onward of the race. This, at least, was the view of a young radical, now dead, who, when he was a little more than thirty, delivered one of the most famous lectures in American history, in the last paragraph of which I find sentences like these:

> Young men of the fairest promise, who begin life upon our shores, inflated by the mountain winds, shined upon by all the stars of God, find the earth below not in unison with these but are hindered from action by the disgust which the principles on which business is managed inspire, and turn drudges, or die of disgust, some of them suicides. What is the remedy? . . . Patience—patience; with the shadows of all the good and great for company; and for solace the perspective of your own infinite life; and for work the study and the communication of principles, the making these instincts prevalent, the conversion of the world.

You will find these sentences on the last page of "The American Scholar" by Ralph Waldo Emerson, written a hundred thirty-two years ago. Or, if you prefer an older mandate, I commend to you the great verse in Micah which reads: "What doth the Lord require of thee, but to do justly, and to love mercy, and walk humbly before thy God?"

87

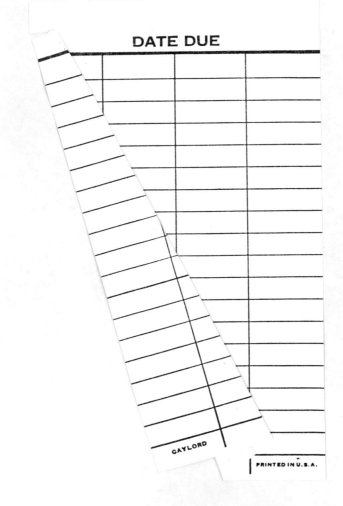

DATE DUE

GAYLORD

PRINTED IN U.S.A.